ISBN 978-0-9559877-1-7

Programming Dynamic Websites Using ASP

Written by Mike Young

INDEX

INDEX

Who should use this book?

This book can be used by many people such as:

▶▶ A student who wishes to learn a computing language.

▶▶ A teacher/lecturer can teach a whole class with structured learning lessons.

▶▶ This book can be used as part of a computing course such as a BTEC in Computing or HNC/HND in Computing.

The only pre-requisite you will need is familiarisation of the HTML language. This book gives the support needed to ensure you can understand and continue this language with confidence. If you want a career in IT, learning ASP will give you a skill many companies are needing to fulfil their website creations.

How to use this book?

▶▶ Although this book is sectioned into 4 parts called 'Days', it does not mean that you need to finish the book in 4 days! This book, if used as part of a course, could take between 18-60 hours to fully understand and re-create the lessons within, depending on your level of understanding.

▶▶ Having an idea for a website can be helpful as you can adjust the scripts to suit your particular project

▶▶ These lessons only show the bare bones and can be part of an assignment that may be part of a larger website.

Ideas you may want to use are : -

Airport Parking	Newsagent	Nursery	Garage	Travel Agent
Coach Hire	Mail Order Business	Driving School	Dating Agency	Social Club
Sports Club	Car Rental	Employees	Builder	Vet

Start off with a simple project and get it working first, you can always add extra parts to this after. Always plan your website on paper, it's easier!

Prelude

About me

My name is Mike Young and I have been an IT lecturer/teacher for around 12 years in various schools/colleges in Essex. Throughout my teaching, I have programmed using many popular computing languages. Most of the time I have used small projects to teach students. From that teaching I have seen and understood how beginners who want to program computers like to learn, and by being presented with information they can digest and also understand quickly, and most of all remember for later use.

Some books have masses of writing, and some prefer to get straight into the coding. This book has one small script, and a screen shot on each page to show what's happening. I have found this to be most helpful with students. Many students don't want to read about it, just code it, and see it work. Understanding how it all works and when you would use it comes later. Learn the language, then try to apply it. When you learned French at school, you learned all the words first, then applied it? This book has the same structure, learn the code then apply it.

This book has been written with the learner in mind.

Typing the code is important, many books have the code ready for you, either online or on a CD. If you don't type the scripts by hand you will lose out from being able to understand how to correct mistakes and suchlike.
Error correcting is all part of the learning...

Now to business.........
HTML was fine and still is, but there was a problem.........

ASP stands for Active Server Pages, and is used to connect databases to websites and other such things, for example, to put the current date on every page using only HTML would require a webmaster to manually edit every file, every day. As you can imagine, this would become very tiring for sites with more than five pages.

Webmasters needed a way to have HTML pages created and modified 'on-the-fly' (live), with information which could change weekly, daily, or by the second, or for each and every request/reload of a web page. They needed those pages to be modified automatically, without their constant oversight, and thus was born server side processing and hence server scripting. ASP used along side other languages can be a very powerful option, and learning ASP can be an enjoyable experience, especially with many simple scripts that will encourage you to want to learn more.

What is ASP?

How Does Server Side Scripting Work?

1. When you request information from a database such as 'laptops costing less than £300', then this request is then sent to the server.
2. The server then sees the request and connects to a stored database and runs the search.
3. The results from that search are now sent back to the server.
4. Finally, the server returns the results back to the browser as plain HTML.

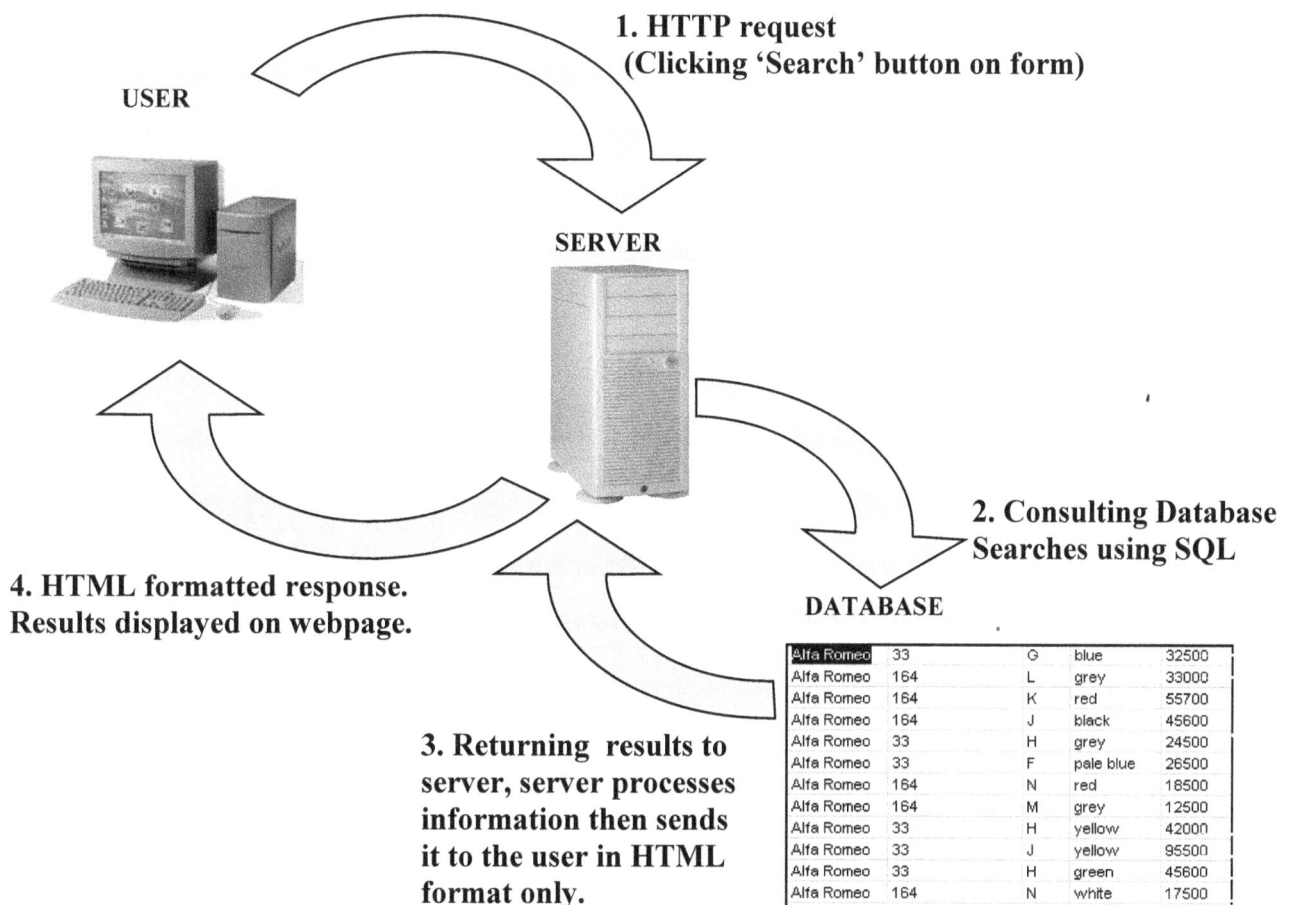

1. HTTP request
(Clicking 'Search' button on form)

USER

SERVER

2. Consulting Database
Searches using SQL

4. HTML formatted response.
Results displayed on webpage.

DATABASE

3. Returning results to server, server processes information then sends it to the user in HTML format only.

Alfa Romeo	33	G	blue	32500
Alfa Romeo	164	L	grey	33000
Alfa Romeo	164	K	red	55700
Alfa Romeo	164	J	black	45600
Alfa Romeo	33	H	grey	24500
Alfa Romeo	33	F	pale blue	26500
Alfa Romeo	164	N	red	18500
Alfa Romeo	164	M	grey	12500
Alfa Romeo	33	H	yellow	42000
Alfa Romeo	33	J	yellow	95500
Alfa Romeo	33	H	green	45600
Alfa Romeo	164	N	white	17500

You can <u>not</u> view ASP code in a browser, you will only see the source as plain HTML. This is because the scripts are executed on the server before the result is sent to the browser. Even if you try to download ASP coded pages it will only ever show the HTML.

The server processes all of the pages and churns this out as HTML only. This would be very easy to get past secure websites otherwise, as the password is in the script when downloaded!!!

This whole action of searching a database is very quick depending on the size of database, still this would be only a few seconds at most.

ASP and other languages

JavaScript

There are many languages you can use with ASP, one of which is JavaScript. To use JavaScript, insert the <script> tags where you need them remembering to end them:

```
<html>
<body>
<%
Response.Write("Hello World!")
%>
<script>
document.write('<p>This is Javascript')
</script>
</body>
</html>
```

Note that - unlike VBScript - JavaScript is case sensitive. You will have to write your ASP code with uppercase letters and lowercase letters when the language requires it.

What's the Difference?

HTML (Hypertext Mark-up Language) has been around ever since the web browser first appeared all those years ago when Tim Berners-Lee first invented it in 1991. HTML went from strength to strength until you really could not do any more with it. Active Server Pages (ASP) took over from where HTML left off in providing the web site creator with the tools and functionality to create rich and truly interactive websites connecting databases and other tricks.

So what are the differences between ASP and HTML? ASP is basically a scripting language that utilises VB Script. You can mix VB Script with HTML to produce web applications that offer an extra step in interactivity. The scripting language (VB Script) is processed by the server and not rendered by the web browser as HTML is. HTML is limited because the web browser must do all the work, in this case, the server is now doing extra work.

ASP is not the only technology that allows you to create these interactive websites. Some of you may have heard about PHP which stands for **PHP: H**ypertext **P**reprocessor, this has the same functionality as ASP but is a little harder to grasp and you are best suited to this if you understand C++ and LINUX. Many people prefer to code in ASP as it can seem simpler to code. PHP requires more knowledge to set up and understand, in my opinion.

4

ASP... What does it do?

So what can you do with ASP?

In a nutshell Active Server Pages allow you to create dynamic forms that can return informative feedback to the user. You can access Microsoft Access Databases via ASP, enabling you to sort database results and add new entries and delete them from a browser. You can update existing content on a website, and you can also remove content. Another excellent use of Active Server Pages is that you can even customize your website depending on which user is viewing it, you could even set up a simple script to welcome the user based on what time of day it is!

ASP gives us a whole new technology which, when used correctly, you can use to implement some truly amazing features like shopping cart systems, information databases, mailing lists, latest news and customized feedback forms. When you program a website with ASP, the programming is executed by the server not the web browser. This gives you increased performance and most importantly allows you to do much more.

The ASP statements are very much like Visual Basic, in fact, VB Script is a cut-down subset of Visual Basic. So if you already know Visual Basic at an application level, moving to ASP will be a quick and painless transition. It does not matter what browser you use, both Firefox and Internet Explorer can be used along with many others, your browser only needs to display HTML.
Active Server Pages are processed by the server so whatever the ASP is, this will create only HTML, so you are sure to know that your web browser will display it correctly.

So what do you need to run an ASP website?

Most importantly your website host will need to support Active Server Pages. There are plenty of service providers popping up each day, however in some cases they can be expensive.

I recommend shopping around for a host because prices do differ and it can save you money by just spending a little time looking around, but a good place to start would be www.redstation.com.

Redstation offers fast ASP hosting, and can cost you as little as £3.95 (which includes free web hosting for a year!), and you will be up and running in approximately 24 hours with a website of your own! You can follow everything in this book except maybe some advanced creation of files as this may need special file permissions not all hosting providers will give you due to security measures. Alternatively all scripts within this book can be run on your own home server/computer if you wish without cost.

Installing ASP on Vista

Does it cost anything?

Asp is free! If you want to test and run it locally you just need to load it on your computer using the Windows CD (usually supplied with your computer).

To use this book you do not need to upload anything, or pay for any website, all you need is a computer and a piece of software loaded from the windows CD. This software is called **Internet Information Services** (**IIS**), this will enable your computer to act as a server, therefore will be able to run ASP scripts.

Installing ASP on Vista

By default, IIS 7.0 is not installed on Windows Vista Home Premium. You can install IIS 7.0 on Windows Vista® Home Premium, Windows Vista® Business, Windows Vista® Ultimate, or Windows Server® 2008.

Below shows the first step which is to open the control panel within Vista's operating system.

Once open you will need to click on **'Turn windows features on/off'**

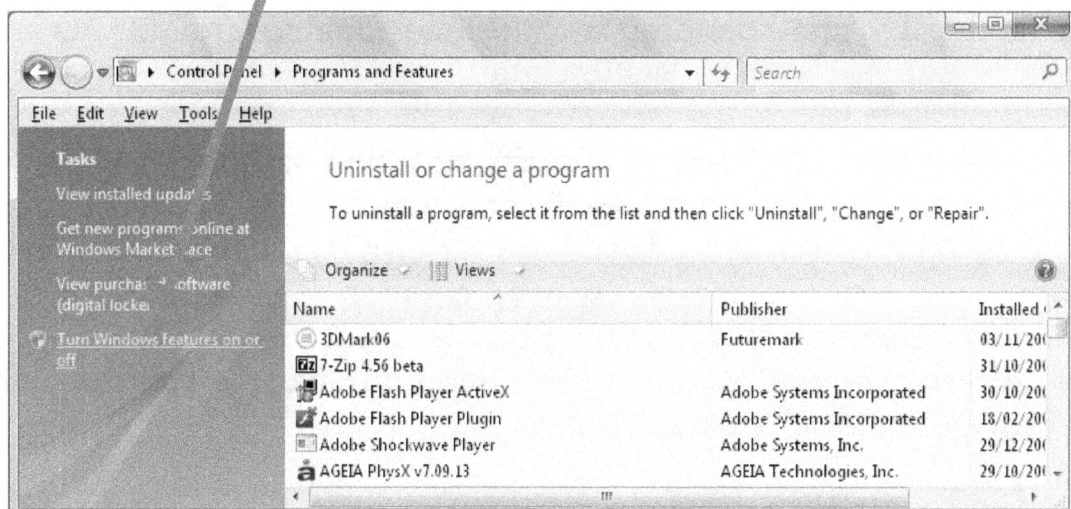

Installing ASP on Vista

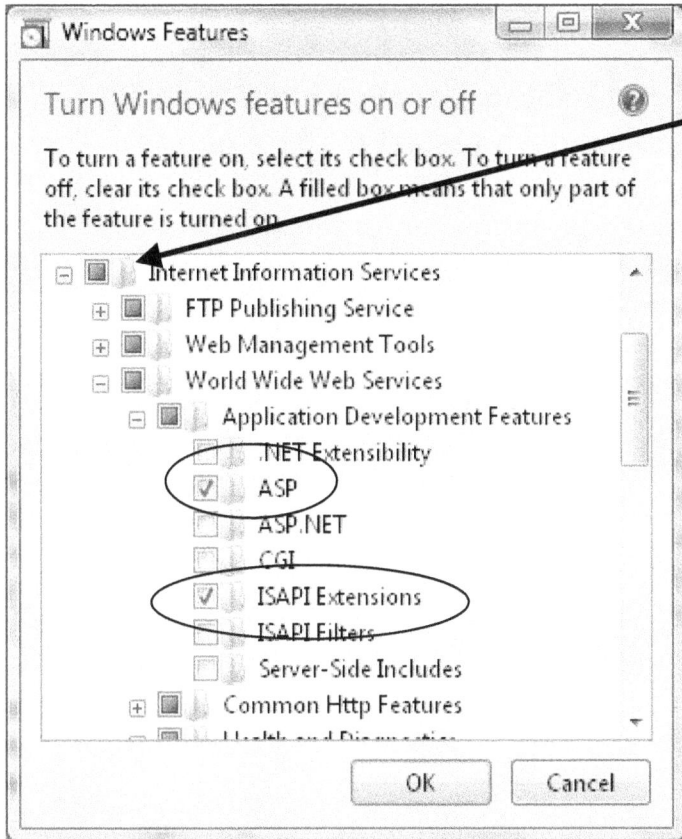

When you get to this stage you are presented with many options.

1. You will need to turn the Internet information services on, by enabling the box. (It will go blue)
2. You will also need to turn on the ASP and ISAPI extensions to enable asp to work on your computer. (use plus buttons)
3. Then click OK

It will then take a few minutes to add this service and display the box below.

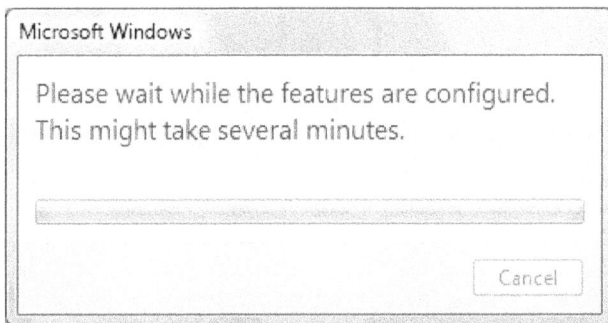

When this has been added to your computer, the box above will have a full green bar and then disappear from your screen.

Once done you now have IIS installed to test this, open a browser and type the name of your computer into the URL bar.
In this case it was Infinity.
You can also use Http://localhost/
You are now ready to start the tutorials.

Have fun......

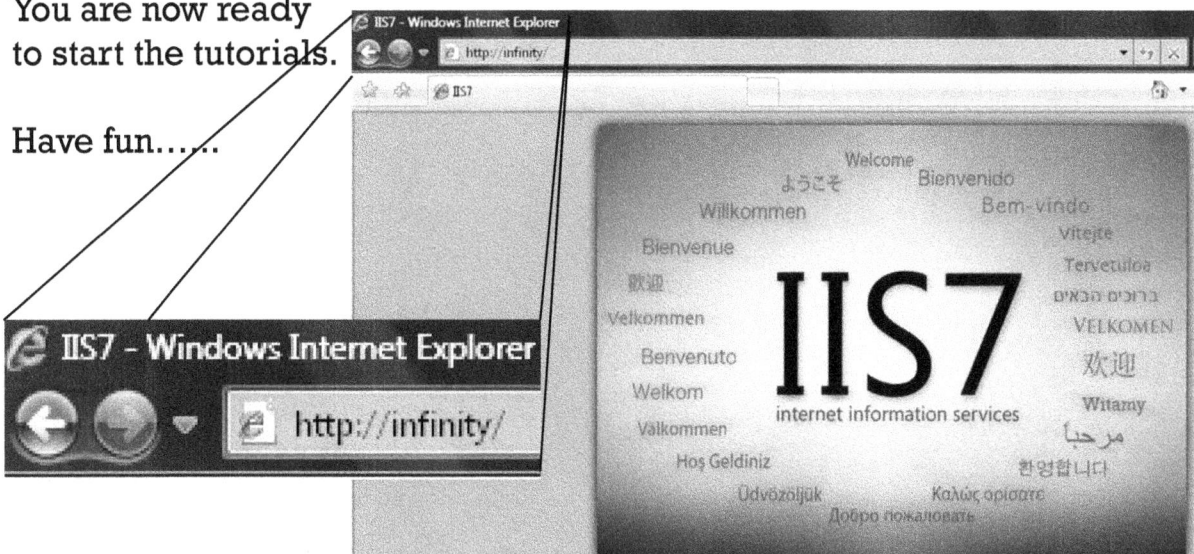

Restarting the Server Vista

A lot of problems are usually solved by one thing, a restart of the web server, if things are not appearing when they should be, a restart may be needed. This should only be done in the beginning stages.

This is found in the
Control panel > Administrative tools > Internet Information Services

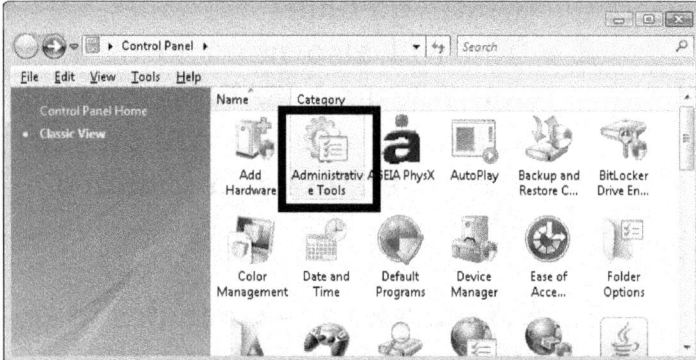

Vista has bunched all the controls together, which is easier, but you can easily change the wrong thing and this may cause your website not to display.

If you don't go changing things, you should be ready to run out of the box!

You do not need to visit this area once it is all set up. You will only open these areas if you experience problems.

Various problems like the asp extension not being understood and executing scripts is common. Sometimes a complete un-install and then a re-install of ASP can also solve most problems.

To restart your server you can use the controls as outlined here

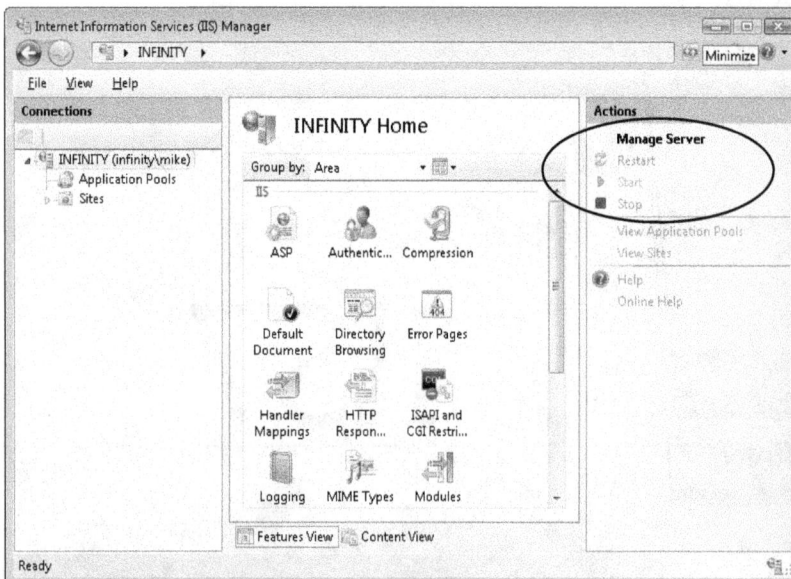

To stop your website processing ASP scripts and to stop the outside world viewing the website that you are hosting, you would stop the server from running, this would then prevent your website from being seen.

Installing ASP on XP

To write ASP pages, you don't need to have an ISP or anyone host your website, this can be done by you...

Thankfully, Microsoft have produced a product called IIS which allows you to explore and work with ASP on your home computer. This is ideal when writing your website at home, until it is time to launch it. In the following pages we will be starting the learning process of a whole new language that will open up your coding skills to the max. You can use the skills shown to create large websites with ease.

Installing IIS on Windows XP Professional
(**Note:** You cannot run ASP on Windows XP Home Edition, unless you use extra software.)

Step One:

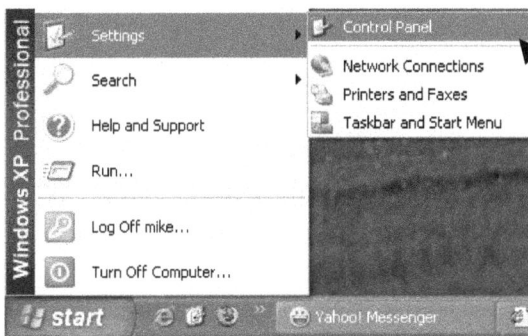

Insert the Windows XP Professional CD-Rom into your CD-Rom Drive, and ignore any auto boot screens that may show.

Click the **Start menu** and then navigate to **Settings** then click **control panel.**

Step Two:

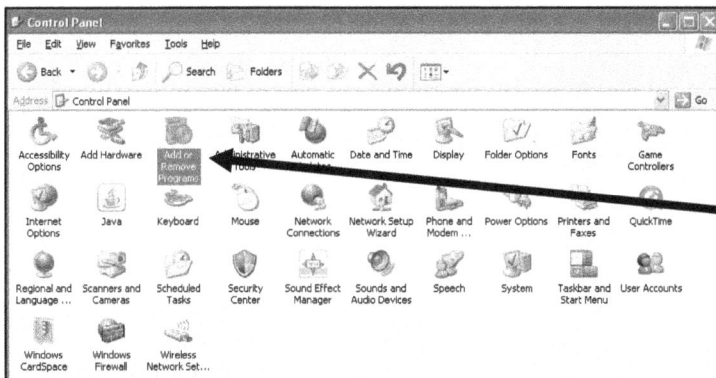

Click the **add/remove programs** icon

Step Three:

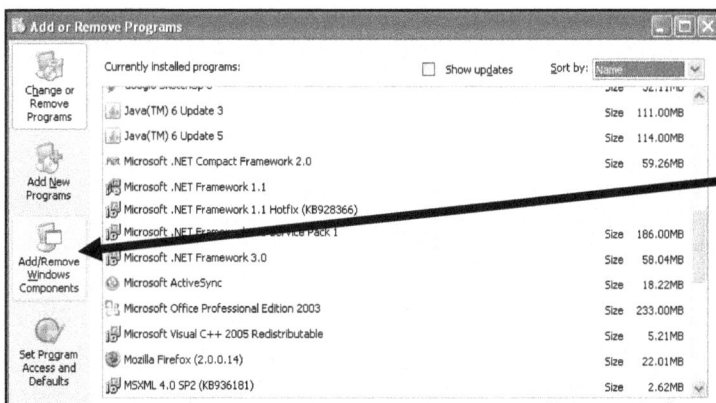

Select the **Add/Remove Windows Components** icon from the left part of the window.

Installing ASP on XP

Step 4:

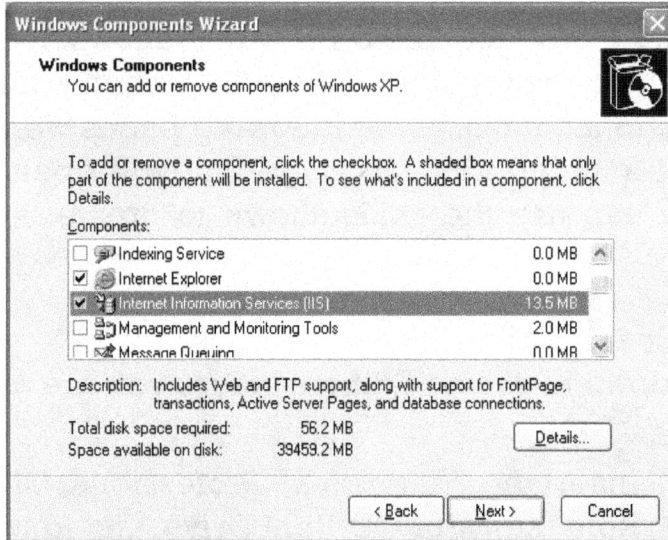

The tick box of **Internet Information Services** will be empty at this stage, you will need to select it. And click **Next**

Step 5:

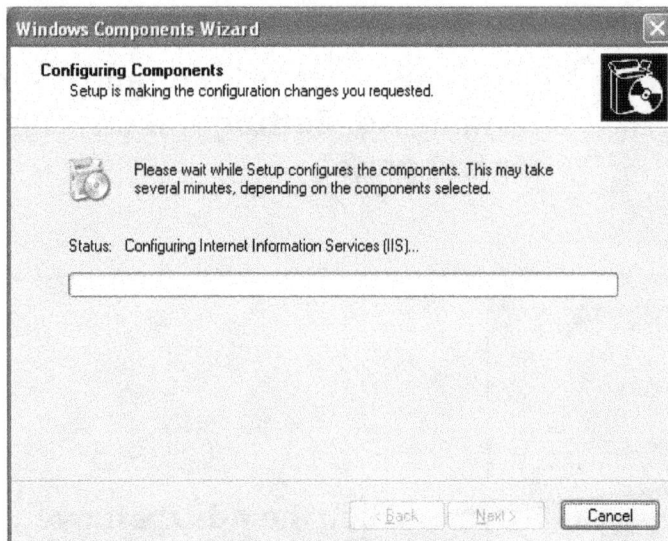

IIS will now configure on your computer, this will take a few minutes.

Step 6:

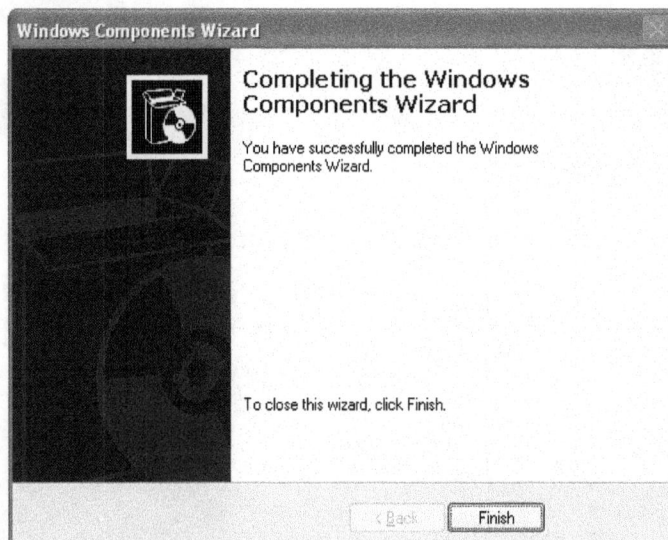

IIS is now installed on your computer, ready to use.
All you need to do now is test it. (Page 14)

Restarting the Server XP

A lot of problems are usually solved by one thing, a restart of the web server, if things are not appearing when they should be, a restart may be needed. This should only be done in the beginning stages.

This is found in the Control panel > Administrative tools > Services.

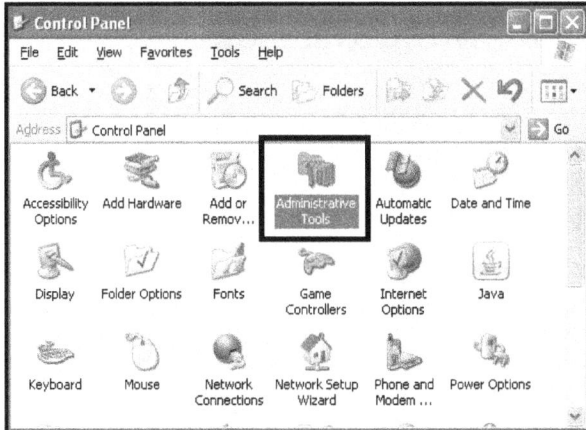

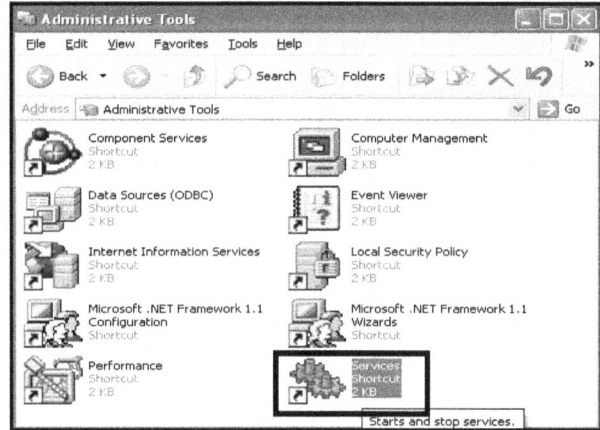

Right mouse button on the 'IIS Admin service', and select restart.
The IIS service will now be restarted within about 30 seconds.

Various problems like the asp extension not being understood and executing scripts is common. Sometimes a complete un-install and then a re-install of ASP can also solve most problems.

To stop your website processing ASP scripts and to stop the outside world viewing your website that you are hosting, you would stop the IIS from running.

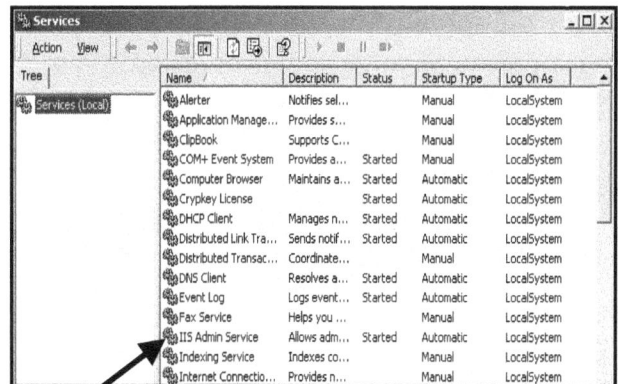

IIS

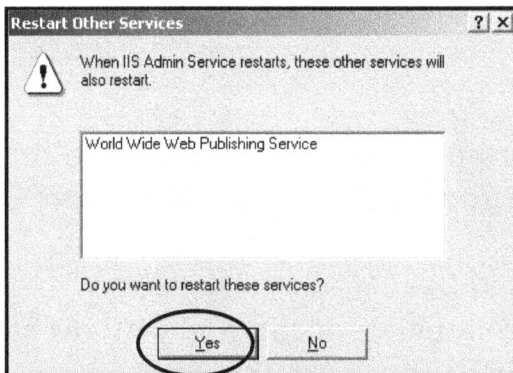

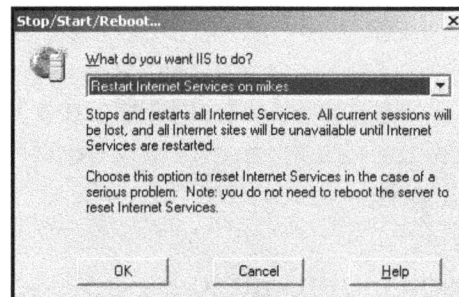

These two screens (right) show what happens when the website restarts, there really isn't too much more to installing and using ASP.

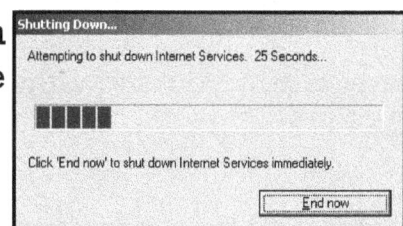

File Extensions

The process is virtually the same within Vista as it is in XP

There are a lot of small problems that can happen still, one of them is that the extension of the file is not showing as test1.asp and instead the operating system chooses to show the file without the extension. It can be a tricky one, but never the less an important one.

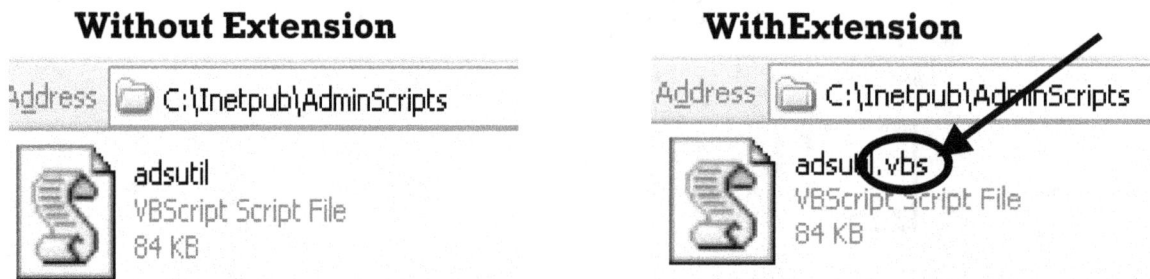

Without Extension

Address C:\Inetpub\AdminScripts

adsutil
VBScript Script File
84 KB

WithExtension

Address C:\Inetpub\AdminScripts

adsutil.vbs
VBScript Script File
84 KB

To correct this select **'Tools'** from a folder window and select **'Folder Options'**

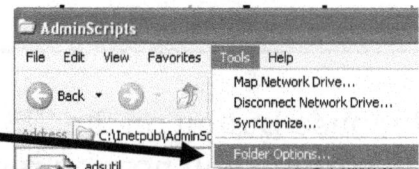

Select the second tab, **'View'**

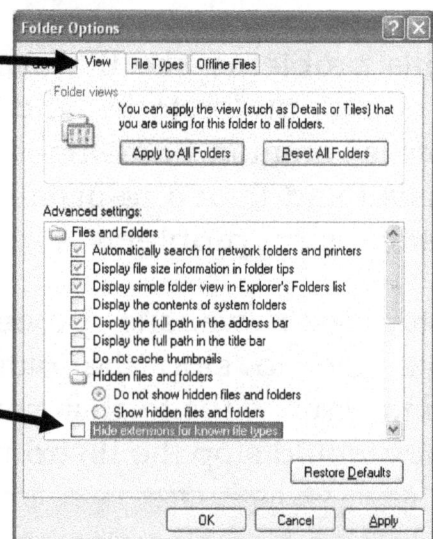

Then select : -
'Hide extensions for known file types'
And **un-tick** the box.

If you ever cut and paste from a PDF file or word document, be aware that the speech marks can change and not work. You will need to type them in by hand again.

It is very important to be able to see the extension of the file you are saving or creating.   If you have the extension hidden it can be the case where a file is named "index.asp.asp". The only thing you would see is "index.asp"!
Only when you show the extension, can it be corrected to only having one file extension.

Configuring ASP XP

By default you do not need to adjust any of the next page , only do so if you are experiencing problems. To adjust the settings of your self hosted website you can enter the configuration area of IIS.

This is inside the '**Control panel**' and then into '**Administrative Tools**'.
From here select **Internet Information Services**.

You will be presented with the screen as above, right mouse button on '**Default Web site**' and select '**properties**'.
This will bring up the next screen as shown on the right.

Select the '**Home Directory**' tab

Directory browsing should not be enabled as this means people can view a whole directory at a time. Not good for a secure website, as people can download ASP scripts looking for passwords etc.

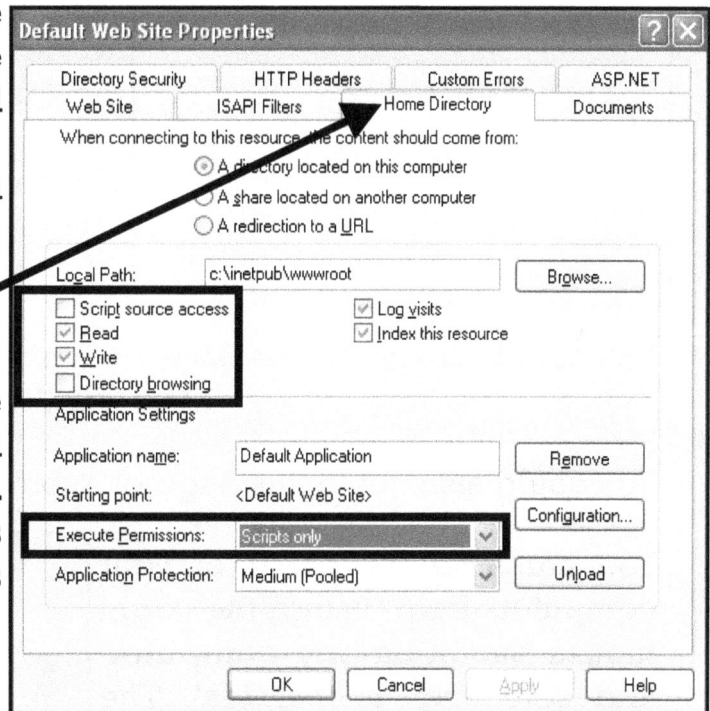

This screen shows lots of options, don't be tempted to change lots of things as this can cause errors.

You must have read and Write selected and also where it says
'Execute Permissions' this should say 'Scripts only'. Everything else leave and all should work. If it does not then this is one area to come back and check all is correct.

You can also restart IIS from here too. By right mouse clicking on the website name then select 'restart'.

Testing ASP

How to test IIS and run an ASP script on Windows XP Professional and Vista

After installing IIS you will find that a set of folders and files have been placed in your C: drive. It should now resemble the screenshot below.

Using Notepad write some ASP code as written below.

```
<%
response.write ("Testing ASP")
%>
```

Save the file as **"test1.asp"** in the **"C:\Inetpub\wwwroot"** folder

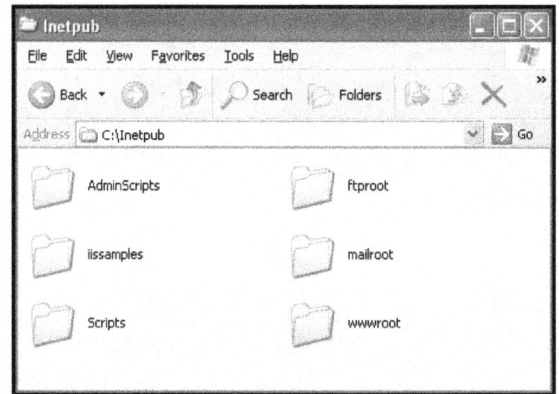

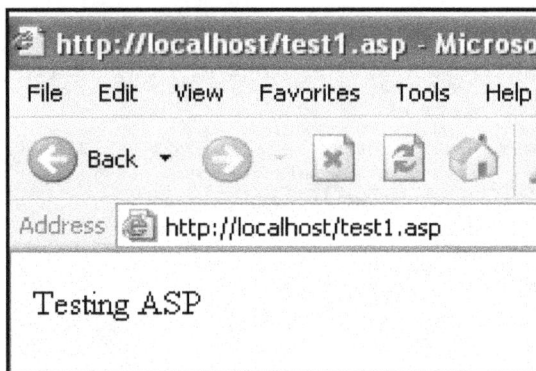

Open your browser and type in
http://localhost/test1.asp
to view your first ASP Page, you should see the screen on the left....

You could also get to this page by typing
http://127.0.0.1/test1.asp

You could also get to this page by typing in the name of the computer.
http://mikes/test1.asp

You could also get to this page by typing **http://localhost/test1.asp**

You can find the name of your computer from using the right mouse button on '**my computer**' and selecting '**properties**'. The screen to the right will appear. As you can see '**mikes**' is this computers name, yours will be different. You can change this by selecting '**Change**'

95% of the time, if you cant get this page to work, it's usually a spelling error.

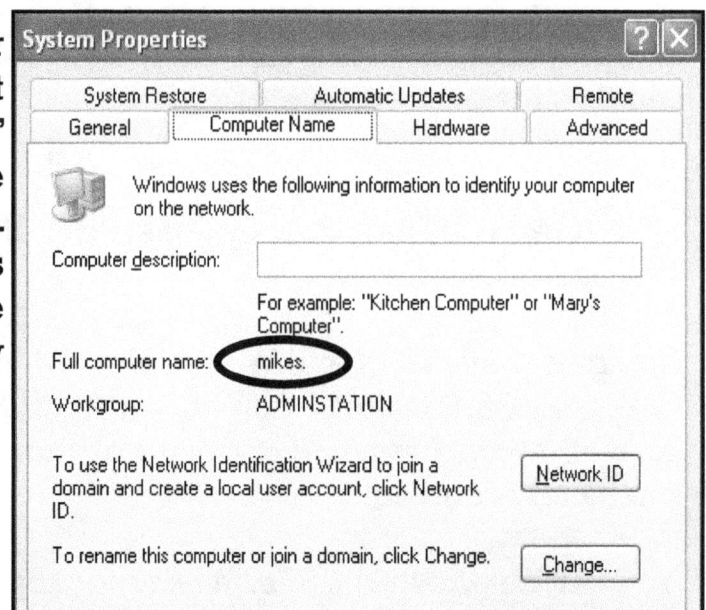

Day 1

- ▸ Learning the basic's
- ▸ Passing data from page to page
- ▸ Handling variables
- ▸ Sessions

This first section is a must! Do not skip this section.

When would you use this coding?
You need to learn well the coding in this first part, as it forms the main structures of ASP. You will use this coding many times, and is your ABC of the ASP world. Many of these scripts perform basic functions of code such as loops, handling variables and starting functions.

Learn, study and practice...

Writing ASP code

Step1.html

```
<html><head>
<title>little steps</title>
</head>
<body>
<h1>Welcome to my website
<br>Hope you have fun!
<h1/>


<%
response.write ("Wizards and spells")
response.write ("<br>")
%>
</body>
</html>
```

Results: -

```
little steps - Microsoft Internet Explorer
File   Edit   View   Favorites   Tools   Help
  Back  ▼          ✖  🔄  🏠   🔍 Search  ☆ Favorites
Address  🔗 http://mikes/book/day1/step1.html

Welcome to my website
Hope you have fun!
```

This file has an extension of .html, the asp will not run as it has not found the .asp extension.
'Wizards and spells' does not show on the webpage, as it has not processed any asp. You will notice that when this page was a html page, it will not execute any asp.

Change the extension to .asp and run it again, you will notice the difference.

16

Writing ASP code

From now on the **<html>** **<head>** **<title>** and **<body>** tags will be taken out as they are not needed.
When making a website for uploading, replace them back in.
The '**<%**' is the start of your ASP. End this by using the '**%>**'.

Step2.asp

```
<h1>
Welcome to my website <br>
with comments hidden</h1>

<%
' you cant see this
%>

This you can see
<comment>This is hidden too</comment>
```

Results: -

This script just shows certain ways of commenting code out, this is very helpful when understanding what a long spagetti script is actually doing, and you may be less confused when coming back to it a while later.

To hide code in ASP it is very easy!
Always try to comment your code, it will be easier for you to understand.

Introducing Variables

Vars.asp

```
<%
dim name
name="mike"
response.write ("My name is" & name)
%>
```

The naming of variables should be a simple one, try to give them a descriptive name, and do not use characters like < & * + , just letters, and letters ending with numbers. It is not case sensitive (hooray), so 'name' could have been called 'NaMe'.

Results: -

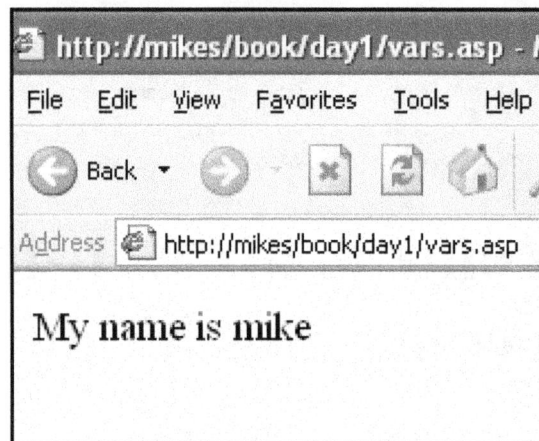

I have declared a variable name, in other words reserved a space called 'name'. This is now used to store any letter or number or sequence for example 'mike'.

Redo this script adding your own name and a different variable name.

Retrieving form values

Count.html

```
<form action="count2.asp" method="post">
<input type=text name=box1>
<input type=submit>
```

Address http://mikes/book/day1/count.html

| Mike | Submit Query |

This code is the start of how we pass a value from one page to another, as you can see in the code there is a property of 'form' called 'action', this determines where the information will be sent, in this case it is count2.asp.

The second property here is action and it can be either POST or GET. We are going to deal with POST for this exercise.

Count2.asp

```
The information passed to this form was
<%
name=request.form("box1")
response.write(name)
%>
```

Results: -

Address http://mikes/book/day1/count2.asp

The information passed to this form was box1=Mike

Type something in the boxes and click submit, see what happens. The key is remembering that **POST** is with **FORM** and that **GET** is with **QUERYSTRING**.
You will learn this soon...

Look at the receiving page to try to figure out what is happening, then try a page yourself.

Retrieving form values

Get1.html

Address http://mikes/book/day1/get1.html

Mike | Submit Query

```
<form action="get2.asp"
method="get">
<input type=text name=box1 >
```

Get2.asp

```
<%
name=request.querystring("box1")
response.write(name)
%>
```

NOTE: Whatever you type in the box will be sent to the next page. You should see by now this is a simple fact of getting your naming right. Syntax errors account for most of non working websites on the internet.

Results: -

As you can see you should never use this for passwords or secure data...

Address http://mikes/book/day1/get2.asp?box1=Mike

Mike

This script is using the second method GET, this will send the information in the url, this is not very good for secure websites as it will send a password uncoded this way.

Test this out and see if you can send a piece of information using the get method.

Retrieving form values

Get3.asp

```
<form action="get3.asp" method="get">
<input type=text name="box1" >
<input type=submit><p>

<%
name=request.querystring("box1")
response.write(name)
%>
```

Submitting to the same page is common, but can cause lots of problems. It is not always needed but can be very handy and loads very quickly!!!

Gain confidence in passing values from page to page, ASP relies on it heavily. If you get this wrong you will have major problems.

Results: -

When objects appear on the same submitted page it appears faster as the page has already been loaded.

Try this using the post method. You will need to change a few bits of coding. Method will become 'POST', and 'request.querystring' will become 'request.form'.

Retrieving form values

Varcount.html

```
<form action="varcount2.asp" method="post">
<input type=text name=box1 >
<input type=text name=box2 >
<input type=submit>
```

Varcount2.asp

```
<%=request.form%><p>
<%=request.form.count%><p>
<%="hello"%><p>
<%response.write "hello again" %>
```

The '.count' part counts how many variables are being sent. If you see '<%=' this will work in the same way that response.write does, and prints to the screen. Lines 3 and 4 do the same thing in different ways.

Results: -

Address	http://mikes/book/day1/varcount2.asp

box1=Cat+&box2=Dog

2

hello

hello again

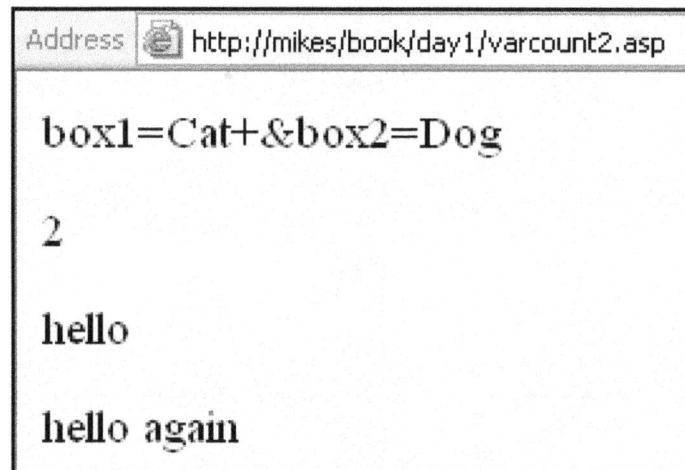

This script shows what information has been passed and also how many pieces of information has been passed, or rather collected.

Tip: - Never trust cut and pasted coding, as speech marks do not cut and paste well.

Retrieving form values

Textarea.html

```
<form action="textarea2.asp" method="post">
<textarea name="ta"></textarea>
<input type=submit>
```

Address http://mikes/book/day1/textarea.html

```
Hello my name is
Mike|
```
Submit Query

Textarea2.asp

```
<%
ta=request.form("ta")
response.write(ta)
%>
```

You should be able to understand the information in the textbox is passed by the variable named '**ta**'.

Results: -

Address http://mikes/book/day1/textarea2.asp

Hello my name is Mike

This script is exactly the same as the previous except it's a textarea. The variable 'ta' is printed to the screen.

Try a combination of the previous scripts, or submit it to itself. Be careful when naming variables as some names are reserved and you will not be able to use.
I reguarly use dog, cat, fish and bird when testing as it easy to distinguish them from coding.

Passwords & Security

Password.html

```
<form action="password2.asp" method="post">
Name  <input type=text name=box1 ><P>
Password  <input type=text name=box2 >
<input type=submit>
```

Password2.asp

```
<%
user=request.form("box1")
password=request.form("box2")
if user="mike" and password="dog" then
response.write("welcome")

else

response.write("Go away")
end if
%>
```

Results: -

Address	http://mikes/book/day1/password.html

Name MIKE

Password LETMEIN   Submit Query

Address	http://mi

Go away

This is a standard 2 page password script. The security that is present here is the way ASP is parsed, or stripped, the user will never get to see the coding due to when it reaches the browser it has already been processed and only pure html is viewable.

Make your own password work in this script.

24

Passwords & Security

Password3.html

```
<form action="password4.asp" method="post">
<table border=0>
<tr><td align="right"> Login:<TD><Input type="text"
name="login"></tr>
<tr><td align="right"> Password:<td><input type="password"
name="password"></tr>
<tr><td align="right"><td><input type="submit" value="Login">
<input type="reset" value="Reset"></tr>
</table></form>
```

Password4.asp

```
<%
If Request.Form("login") = "mike" AND Request.Form("Password") =
"monday26" Then
      Response.Redirect "index2.html"
Else
      Response.Redirect "index3.html"

      Response.End
End If
%>
```

Results: -   **(Note: Index2.html and Index3.html are just plain text files)**

Address	http://mikes/book/day1/password3.html

Login:	mike
Password:	****
	Login Reset

password accepted	**index2.html**

entry failed! Please try again	**index3.html**

This script checks to see if a user has input the right password and then redirects them to the correct page.

Is the password case sensitive?

Maths and ASP

Adding.html

```
<form action="adding2.asp" method="get">
<input type=text name=box1 >
<input type=text name=box2 ><br>
<input type=submit>
```

Address http://mikes/book/day1/adding.html

| 12 | 33 |

Submit Query

Adding2.asp

```
<%
box1=request.querystring("box1")
box2=request.querystring("box2")

ans=cint(box1)+cint(box2)
response.write(ans)
%>
```

Results: -

Address http://mikes/book/day1/adding2.asp?box1=12&box2=33

45

This uses the cint function

This script is simple to understand, if the cint function is not used and two variables are added, the result will be in this case 99, it adds or rather places the values together without actually adding them.
This script uses the **cint** function.
There are lots of other maths functions, experiment with them, but there's not enough time to explain them all.

Add a third box, and add all the amounts up.

26

Conditional Statements (CASE)

Case.html

```
<form action="case2.asp" method=post>
<select name="ship">
<option>land</option>
<option>sea</option>
<option>air</option>
</select>
<input type=submit></form>
```

Case2.asp

```
<%
varship = request.form("ship")
select case varship
case "land"
        response.write("shipping by land costs £3.50")
case "sea"
        response.write("shipping by sea costs £5.70")
case "air"
        response.write("shipping by air costs £12.00")
end select
%>
```

Results: -

Address	http://mikes/book/day1/case.html
sea ▼ Submit Query	
land	
sea	
air	

Address	http://mikes/book/day1/case2.asp
shipping by sea costs £5.70	

The text from the option is selected is sent in the variable named 'ship', this is then received by the next page and transerred into the variable named 'varship'. This script is a time saver instead of using if and else statements. There may be many choices that could be made, and case could be the best answer.

Make your own case statement for your favourite foods.

Conditional Statements (ELSEIF)

Exam1.html

```
<form action="exam2.asp" method="get">
<input type=text name="test" >
<input type=submit>
```

Exam2.asp

```
<%
test=request.querystring("test")
dim exam
 IF test > 90 THEN
    exam = "A"
 ELSEIF test > 80 THEN
    exam = "B"
 ELSEIF test > 70 THEN
    exam = "C"
 ELSEIF test > 60 THEN
    exam = "D"
 END IF
response.write(exam)
%>
```

Results: -

| 78 | Submit Query |

C

Here is what is called an 'if' statement. This is used very much in all programming languages. You could explain this by saying ' If sunny then sunglasses, if raining then umbrella, if cold then coat.

Make a Note ...

If you noticed, END IF is two words but ELSEIF is only one word.

Change this script as there is a problem with it for numbers less than 60!!!

Conditional Statements (FOR & DO LOOP)

Next.asp

```
<%
dim i
for i=1 to 50
response.write "The number is " & i &  "<br>"
next
%>
```

Doloop.asp

```
<%
DIM counter
DO UNTIL counter = 10
Counter = Counter + 1
response.write("<br>This is number")
response.write(counter)
LOOP
%>
```

Results: -

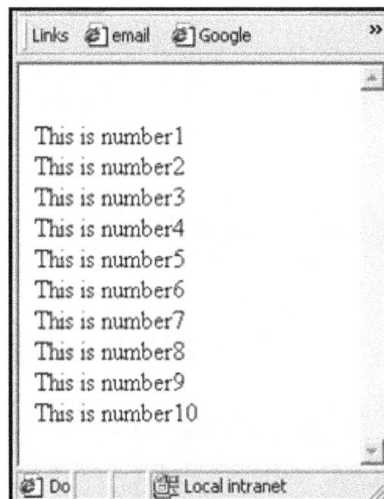

Looping is very common in programming and it is there so we do not have to write lots of coding again and again. We can repeat it as many times as we like.

Add to this script, and change the numbers. Maybe try the times tables.

Conditional Statements (CASE again!)

Day.asp

```
<%
dim weekday
weekday = datepart("w", date)
select case weekday
case 1, 2, 3
response.write("Mon-Wed")
case 4,5
response.write("Thursday or Friday")
case 6, 7
response.redirect "weekend.html"
end select
%>
```

Weekend.html

```
<h1>It's the weekend, Hooray!!!</h1>
```

Results: -

If run between a Monday and Wednesday.

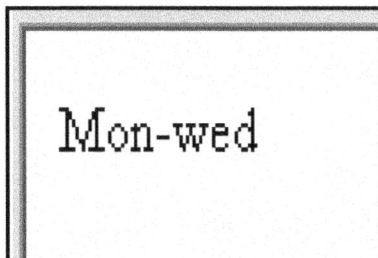

Mon-wed

If run on a Saturday or Sunday.

Address http://mikes/book/day1/weekend.html

It's the weekend, Hooray!!!

This has an intelligent part to it, it takes the number of the weekday and places this into the variable called 'weekday'. Then it is used in a case statement, and depending on the day it will perform a different action each time. This is good for changing content on a web page to make people think you update it a lot!

You will need to change the day on the computer using the date and time properties to test the other answers to this script. (Double-click the time, bottom right hand corner, and change the date.)

Time in VBscript

Time.html

```
<script language ="vbscript">
document.write "The year is ", Year(Now())

document.write "<br>The time is ", (time())
document.write ("<br>")
document.write datediff("ww", Now(),"25-dec-03")
document.write " weeks till xmas"
</script>
```

This is not ASP! True, but if you code JavaScript you will
see the likeness of how ASP handles the time element in
the next script. You can use any Visual Basic Script within
ASP pages, they work very well together.

Results: -

Address 🖉 http://mikes/book/day1/time.html

The year is 2003
The time is 23:24:50
45 weeks till xmas

Now try your own Add how many days (d) till your birthday?

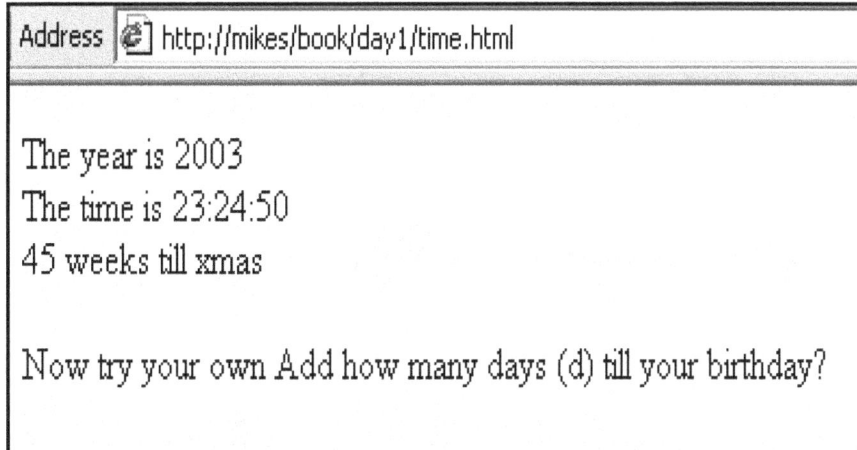

This can show you how easy Vbscript is to use and what
purpose it can serve. Time is difficult to code in other
languages, and is best done in Vbscript.

Work out how you could change the script to show how
many days till your birthday.

Time in ASP

Greeting.asp

```
<%
Dim h
h = hour(now())

response.write("<p>" & now())
response.write(" is the time  now </p>")

If h < 12 then
response.write("Good Morning!")
else
response.write("Good Evening!")
end if
%>
```

The above script is an easy snippet of code to improve, and is easy to understand.

Results: -

```
Address  http://mikes/book/day1/greeting.asp

11/12/2008 1:53:35 PM is the time now

Good Evening!
```

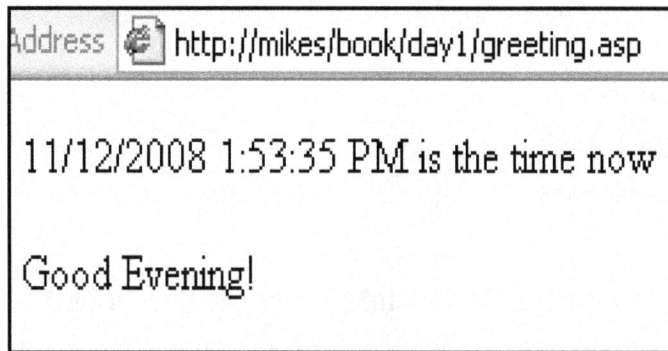

Time in ASP is easy as its Vbscript you use. This script is greeting the user depending on the time of the server. If the server time is less than 12, it will greet with 'Good Morning' and after 12 it will greet with 'Good Evening'.

Try to make your own up, maybe with three time greetings, (clue: -Two **'end if's'** are needed)

Time in ASP

Time2.asp

```
The time now is <%=NOW%>

<%=DATE%>
<%=TIME%>
<%=MONTH(DATE)%>
<%=DAY(DATE)%>
<%=WEEKDAY(DATE)%>
<%=YEAR(DATE)%>
```

One thing to note, the time is the time currently on the server. Therefore, it may differ from the time you see on your own computer.

The easiest and quickest way is **<% =time %>**
Try this in notepad by itself.....

Results: -

```
Address  http://mikes/book/day1/time2.asp ▼

The time now is 15/02/2003 23:40:4315/02/200323:40:4321572003
One thing to note, the time is the time on the server. Therefore, it may
differ from the time you show.


Your task is to make this look better!
```

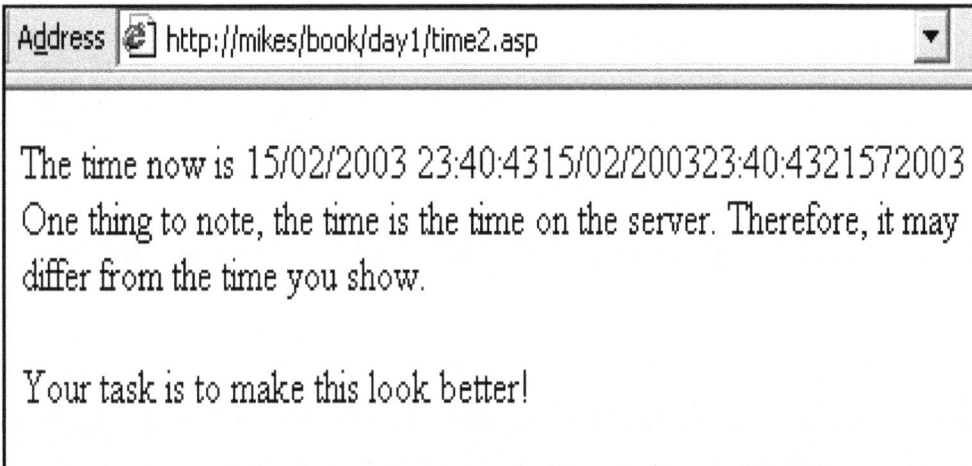

This script shows some of the ways time can be shown in ASP

Your task is to make this look more presentable, only use the parts you need.

Server Variables

Servervars.asp

```
<%= "The web servers name is "%>
<%=request.servervariables("server_name")%>
<p>I am using
<%=request.servervariables("server_software")%>
```

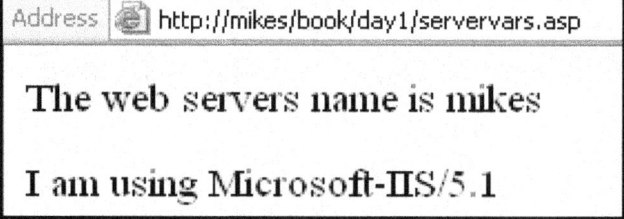

Showallvars.asp

```
<table><tr><td>
<b>Server Variable</b>
<td><b>Value</b></tr>
<% For Each name In Request.ServerVariables %>
<tr><td><%= name %><td>
<%= Request.ServerVariables(name) %></tr>
<% Next %>
</table>
```

Results: -

Test the script above to see what data you can find using ASP.

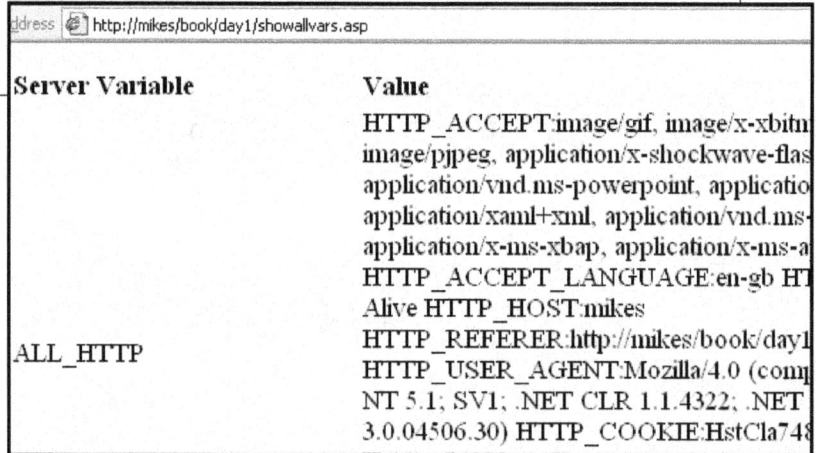

I am using these sever variables to find out information like the browser type so I can send the user to a certain webpage. It can also help track IP addresses for measuring the length of visiting times, and what pages someone browses, but this is usually better handled by some of the free and easy to use visitor tracking websites that produce detailed statistics of your audience who visit your site. You only need to install a small piece of code on your main page for it to start collecting data from visitors.

Try to make the users computer name bold. (<b>)
Time to add HTML, and experiment.....

Server Variables

Showall.asp

```
<%
for each item in request.servervariables
        response.write(item & "<br>")
next
%>
```

Results: -

```
PATH_TRANSLATED
QUERY_STRING
REMOTE_ADDR
REMOTE_HOST
REMOTE_USER
REQUEST_METHOD
SCRIPT_NAME
SERVER_NAME
SERVER_PORT
SERVER_PORT_SECURE
SERVER_PROTOCOL
SERVER_SOFTWARE
URL
HTTP_ACCEPT
HTTP_ACCEPT_LANGUAGE
HTTP_CONNECTION
HTTP_HOST
HTTP_REFERER
HTTP_USER_AGENT
HTTP_COOKIE
HTTP_ACCEPT_ENCODING
```

Use the coding below and any of the server variables to retrieve the information needed.

<%=request.servervariables ("replace me")%>

Although this script is short, it does a lot of work, it shows all the server variables that could be run on the page at the same time. This is more like a reference to server variables than a script you would include on a page for a website.

Use this information to achieve the same results as the print screen below.

Code a script to show the following results : -

```
You are browsing this site with: Mozilla/4.0 (compatible; MSIE 5.5;
Windows 98; Win 9x 4.90)
Your IP address is: 80.1.18.213
The DNS lookup of the IP address is: 80.1.18.213
The method used to call the page: GET
The server's domain name: www.ezetraining.com
The server's port: 80
The server's software: Microsoft-IIS/4.0
```

Random

Random.asp

```
<%
randomize
dim rand1
rand1 = int(rnd*3)+1
if rand1 = 1 then
response.write "its going to be windy!"
elseif rand1 = 2 then
response.write "its going to be sunny!"
elseif rand1 = 3 then
response.write "its going to be raining!"
end if
%>
```

its going to be sunny!

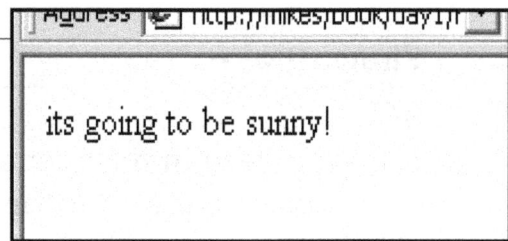

This script is easy to follow, first it picks a random number then assigns it to **rand1**, then depending on what is stored in **rand1** it will show a certain quote. What randomize does is set a seed for random number generation. In short, it gets the ball rolling so that you can generate random numbers.

Add some more quotes in

Server Map Paths

Mappath.asp

```
<%=server.mappath("This is the directory where this is being run from")%>
```

Results: -

Back ▾ | Search | Favorites
Address http://mikes/book/day1/mappath.asp

c:\inetpub\wwwroot\book\day1\This is the directory where this is being run from

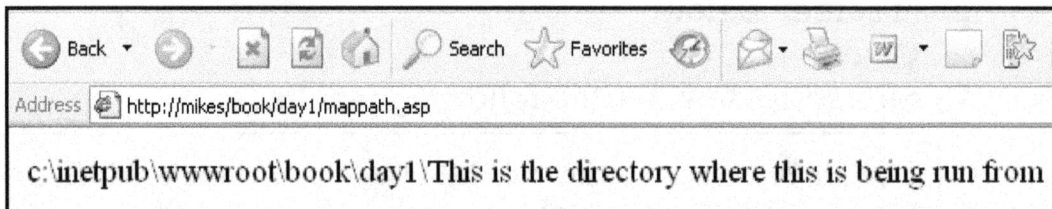

When you are uploading you are never quite sure where to refer to a document unless you can find what level within the root you are. Uploading this script and running it will show you where your scripts are located. This will also make connecting to databases a lot easier.

Running external scripts

Serverexe.asp

```
Welcome to my web site<p>
The time is now
<% server.execute("time.asp") %>
<p> wow this is fun!
```

Time.asp

```
<%=time%>
```

The above file executes (starts) another script within the website and returns the information to the page. In this example it is the time that is displayed.

Results: -

```
Welcome to my web site

The time is now 20:22:02

wow this is fun!
```

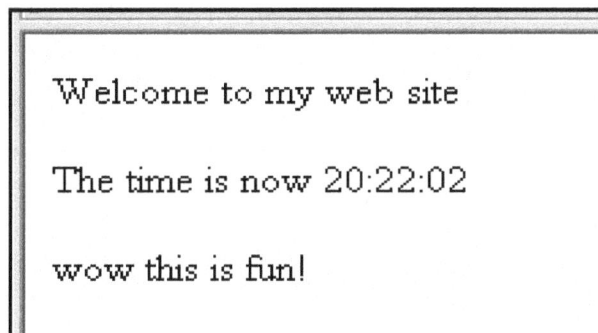

Another example of how you could use this script: -
```
If Request.Form("theaction") = "DeleteForm" then
      Server.Execute ("IncludePages/deleteForm.asp")

ElseIf Request.Form("theaction") = UpdateForm" then
      Server.Execute ("IncludePages/updateForm.asp")
End If
```

Server.Execute() the file can be conditionally included if put in an IF/THEN. They only run if a condition is met.
'Include files' that we meet soon are always run without choice. The effect is similar but this gives greater control of when it happens in the script.

When creating a large database website this scripting can save a lot of coding. One ASP file to delete content, and one ASP file to add content, and so on.

Sessionid.asp

```
My unique session ID is
<%
Response.Write(Session.SessionID)
%>
```

Why do I need a session?

Sessions are a very important part of ASP, these enable a user to log-on to a website and use it for a period of time. After this time has expired the user will have to log-on again. This you will see used in anywhere from online banking sites to shopping online. If a user leaves their computer for a long time and someone else uses it, the sessions should have expired meaning they will not get into passworded areas without permission even if the person has not logged off.

Results: -

Address http://mikes/book/day1/sessionid.asp

4226979

- This session number is a unique one, given to the browser from the server,
- Why is does it have to be unique?
- What function does it have?

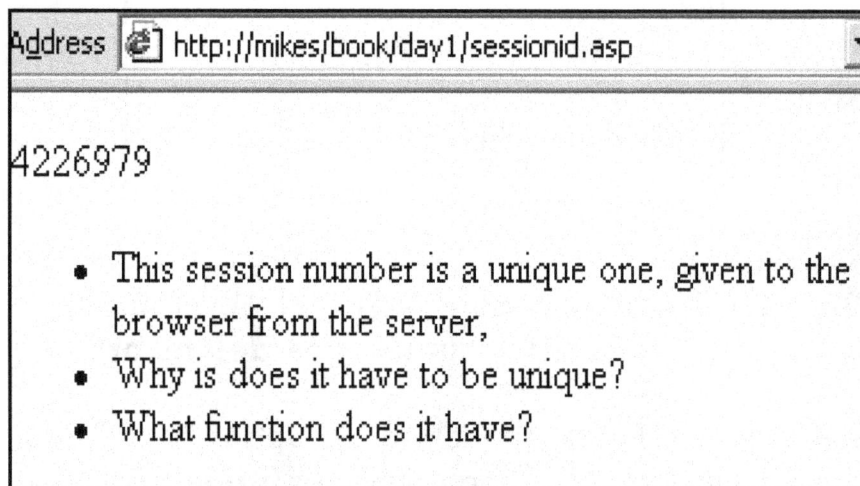

This is the basic version, the next couple of scripts will teach you how you can use these scripts in a website where you would login, again using ASP to search the database for the members details.

This number has to be unique as if it uses the same number twice, it may log off two or more users by accident.

Session1.asp

```
<%
session("page")="dog"
%>
<%
response.write(session("page"))
%>
```

This page writes the word **dog** into a session called **page,** it then asks to print the session to the screen, therefore we end up with the print screen below.

You may still be confused on how to use this script....
The next page shows an example....

Results: -

```
Address  http://mikes/book/day1/session1.asp

dog
```

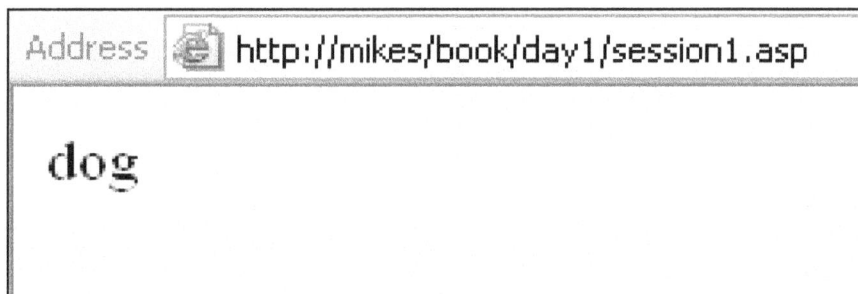

Not much to start with, but little steps.
The session has reserved a variable name called 'page' and within that has saved some text called 'dog'.
The session name called 'Page' now holds the text 'dog'.

Play around with this idea till you become familiar with the way session information is stored.

Rewrite this page using only one set of percent brackets and make two session variables called 'page' and 'name'.

Session3.html

```
<Form action="session4.asp" method="post">
<Table><tr>
<td align="right">Login:
<td><input type="text" name="login">
<tr><td align="right">Password:
<td><input type="password" name="password">
<td><input type="submit" value="Login">
</Table></form>
```

You may notice the table has some HTML missing
(</tr> and </td>) but it will still work.
This will get sent to session4.asp to see if the correct
username and password has been entered, and that will
write an imaginary note that we are allowed to view any
secure places.

Results: -

| Address | http://mikes/book/day1/session3.html |

Login: mike|
Password: [   ] [Login]

Note: No password is needed, you can add this
at a later stage.

Remember that we are setting the users time out at 60
seconds in this next script. Of course in the real world a
user should be logged on for at least 5 minutes. There is
a fine line between hassle for the user and security, this
will all depend on what your system is actually
protecting.

Make sure you have the text boxes correctly named, as
this will mean the script wont receive information from the
previous page.

Session4.asp

```
<%
session.timeout=1
session("username")=request.form("login")
%>Welcome
<%
response.write(session("username"))
%><p>
<a href="session5.asp">Try this after 1 minute</a>
<p> <p><a href="session7.asp">Login to secure
pages</a><p>
<a href="session6.asp">Logout</a>
```

Session5.asp

```
<h1>Your session name is
<%
response.write(session("username"))
%>
</h1>
```

Results: -

Address http://mikes/book/day1/session4.asp

Welcome mike

Login

Session name (Try this after 1 minute, to see if it has timed out)

Look at secure pages

Logout

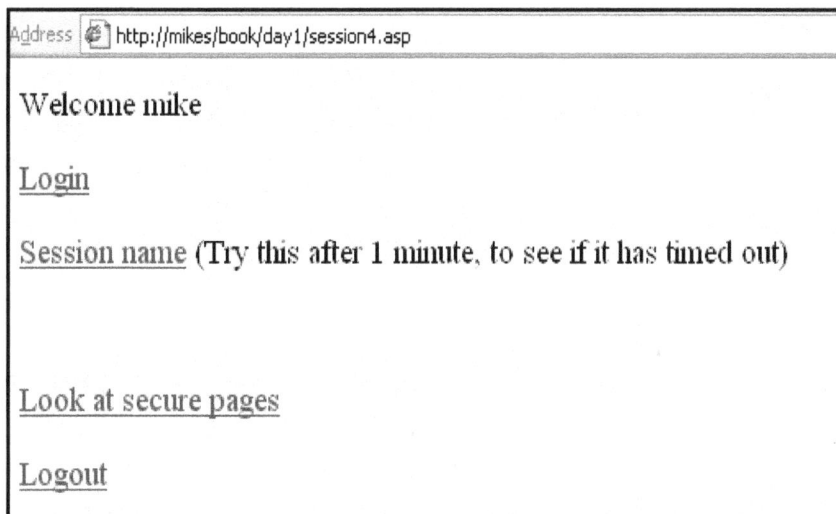

The password section is not used in this example, you could quite easily make this work, as you have been shown this in previous examples.

The username is what is saved as the session variable called *'login'*. At the top of the script there is an instruction to shorten the default time a session lasts, to 1 minute. (**session.timeout=1**). Make sure you leave it for a full minute with no activity.

Sessions 5/6

Session5.asp (within 1 minute)

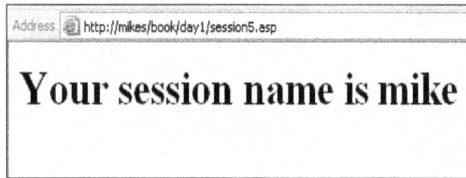

Address http://mikes/book/day1/session5.asp

Your session name is mike

After clicking on the link
'Session name' within the given time of one minute, the session variable stays with us and the server knows that we are still the same user clicking through.

The session data is now shown as **'mike'**.

Session5.asp (after 1 minute)

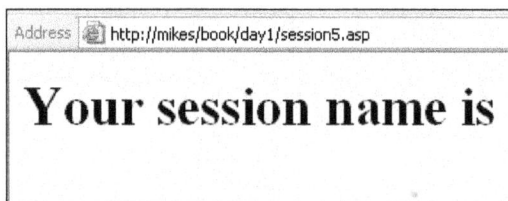

Address http://mikes/book/day1/session5.asp

Your session name is

Now click **'Session name'** after a full 60 seconds to see if it has timed out and forgot the user.

As you can see the results we get after a minute, is very

different. The session name has been erased.

Now any links that need you to be logged in under a session will not work.

Securearea.asp

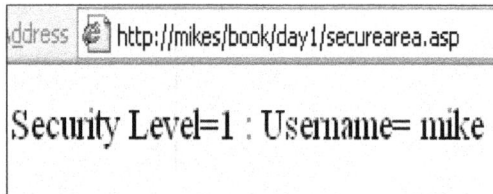

ddress http://mikes/book/day1/securearea.asp

Security Level=1 : Username= mike

This screen show us that our session was recognised, and we were transferred to the secure area (a basic HTML page). Unless our username and password were recognised we would not have got into this area.

Session7.asp

Address http://mikes/book/day1/session7.asp

Disallowed

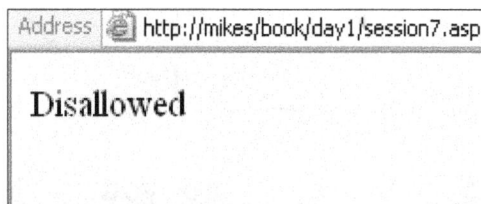

If we wait until the session is timed out and try to access **'look at secure pages'** we get the screen opposite. It cannot find and verify the correct session/user.

After going back to the page with the links, (session4.asp) we now click onto the link that says **'Look at secure pages'**.

This has now gone to another page and displayed a message of **'Disallowed'**.

Session7.asp

```
<%
If session("username")="mike" then
   Response.Redirect "securearea.asp"
response.write "Security Level=1 " & session("page")
end if
If session("username")="dog" then
   Response.Redirect "securearea2.asp"
response.write "Security Level=2" & session("page")
end if
response.write("Disallowed")
%>
```

Securearea.asp

```
<%
response.write "Security Level=1 : Username= " &
session("username")%>
```

Securearea2.asp

```
<%
response.write "Security Level=2 : Username= " &
session("username")%>
```

Results: -

Address	http://mikes/book/day1/securearea.asp
Security Level=1 : Username= mike	

Address	http://mikes/book/day1/securearea2.asp
Security Level=2 : Username= dog	

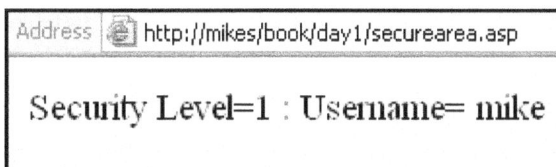

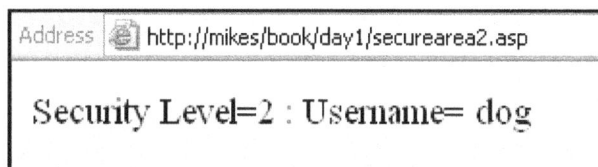

Logged in with '**mike**' and then logged in with '**dog**', and sent to different pages.

This page does quite a few things, firstly it checks if the session variable called username, which was what we logged in as in the username box actually equals 'mike'.
If this is true it then writes to the page Security Level=1 and then the session value of 'page'.
Otherwise if the session value of username equals 'dog' then it will write Security Level=2 and then the session value for 'page'. Anything else will write 'Disallowed' as we have seen on the previous page.

Test this and make small changes.

Include files

Include.asp

```
<!--#include file="stuff.inc"-->
```

Stuff.inc

```
<%
response.write ("Hello I'm actually from an include file")
%>
```

The simplicity of an include file is great, and it can be used for so many uses. You can include whole lots of HTML design for the top of a page and reproduce it in each page using include files. In a way it acts like CSS, pulling the information from somewhere else.

Results: -

Address | http://mikes/book/day2/include.asp

Hello I'm actually from an include file

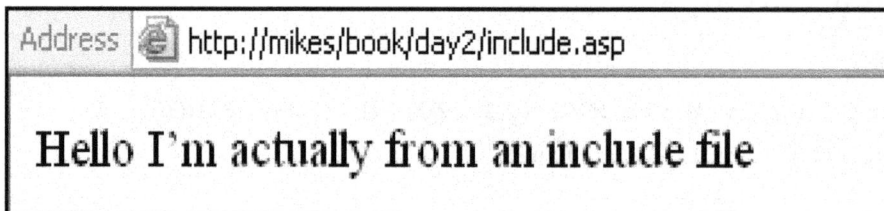

Include files are an easy way of including other files within your ASP page. It can simplify many procedures you have to do within a page. The include option is the heart of making efficient ASP files and re-usable chunks.
It can be used in either of the following ways……

Method 1	**Method 2**
Script	Include file
Include file	Include file
Script	Include file
Include file	Include file
Script	Script

Try to make a page up that uses a picture, and use it from an external include file. Remember to save the include file with the extension **'.inc'**

Day 2

- Creating files 'on the fly'
- Adding text to a file
- Deleting files from a web server by code

When would you use this coding?

You could let users create files themselves to be held online in your web space. These may be like a profile page, these scripts are only made up from skeleton code, another function could be a basic hit counter. Colour, pictures and text will all need to be added at a later date.

This script can be used in conjunction with upload scripts and form part of a Virtual Learning Environment (VLE). Each user can create their home-page and edit parts of their page. Remember this is only the beginning!

Hit counter

Hit.asp

```
<%
Set fs = CreateObject("Scripting.FileSystemObject")
Wfile=server.mappath("\") & "\book\day1\aspcount.txt"
on error resume next
Set a = fs.OpenTextFile(Wfile)
hits = Clng(a.ReadLine)
hits = hits + 1
a.close
if error then
hits = 1
end if
Set a = fs.CreateTextFile(Wfile,True)
a.WriteLine(hits)
a.Close
%>

Number of hits: <% =hits %>
```

Results: -

Address http://mikes/hit.asp

Number of hits: 17

aspcount.txt - Notepad

File   Edit   Format   View   Help

17

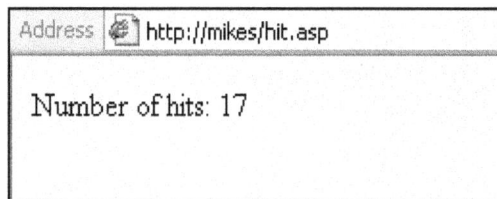

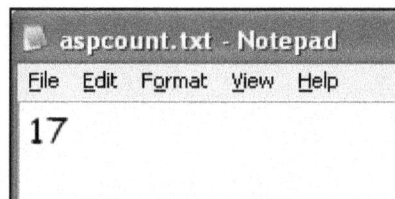

📋 This hit counter is at the most basic it can be, each time the coding is activated, meaning if this text above is placed within a page, it will open a text file, called in this case 'aspcount.txt', once open the server reads the number in the text file then adds 'one' to it, and saves that number to the file. If there is no text file it will create one. The path can be changed of the text file if needed, but try to keep both files together, its easier that way!

📋 This file will change every time someone visits that certain page. You could add a page counter to every page in your website to see which page is most visited, this could be extended by making one page showing all visits of your website. This may be hidden from your visitors, and then shows you where people are going to within your website.

Creating text files

Files.asp

```
<big>Welcome to files and folders in ASP<p>
We will be opening connections and below are helpful num-
bers, <br>try to remember them.<p>
1 =    Read<br>
2 =    Add data<br>
8 =    Append data
<p>
Check your c:/inetpub/book/day2 folder, see if there is file
called 'mikesfile.txt'<br>
If there is delete it, if not we are going to create one in ASP!
<p>
<a href="createfile.asp">Lets create</a>
```

Results: -

Address http://mikes/book/day2/files.asp

Welcome to files and folders in ASP

We will be opening connections and below are helpful numbers,
try to remember them.

1 = Read
2 = Add data
8 = Append data

Check your c:/inetpub/book/day2 folder, see if there is file called 'mikesfile.txt'
If there is delete it, if not we are going to create one in ASP!

Lets create

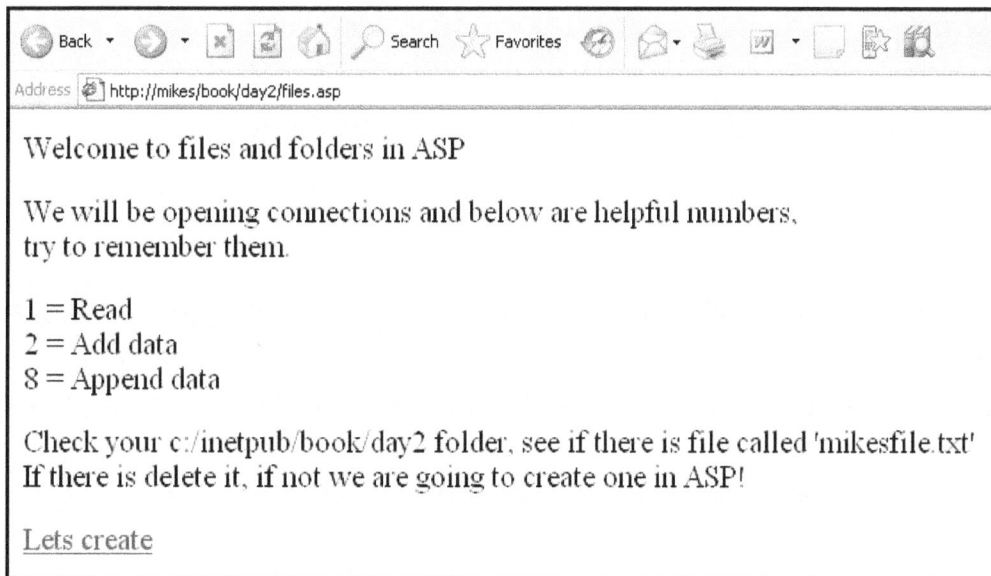

This technique can be useful in certain ways, it can be tailored to your liking and use, depending on what you need it to do. This is just the bare bones of the coding that is working, no unnecessary text. This first file only sets up the page and creates a link to the file. This will create a text file called 'mikesfile.txt' that will now be created physically on the web server.

It will be viewable from a net connection by url, unless it has security placed upon it. Be warned! Do not use this type of storage for sensitive data, and before you do launch any security for a web site, make sure you test it fully first.

Creating text files

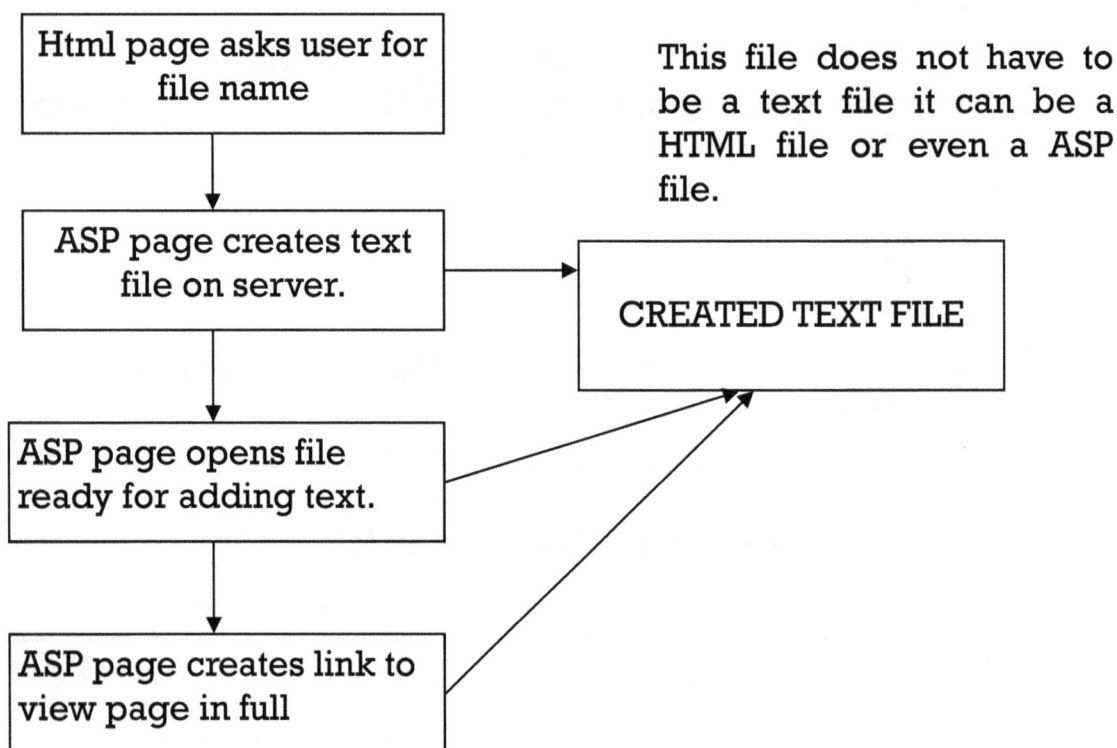

```
┌──────────────────────────┐
│ Html page asks user for  │
│        file name         │
└──────────────────────────┘
             │
             ▼
┌──────────────────────────┐          This file does not have to
│ ASP page creates text    │─────┐     be a text file it can be a
│ file on server.          │     │     HTML file or even a ASP
└──────────────────────────┘     │     file.
             │                   │
             ▼                   ▼
┌──────────────────────────┐   ┌──────────────────────────┐
│ ASP page opens file      │   │                          │
│ ready for adding text.   │───│   CREATED TEXT FILE      │
└──────────────────────────┘   │                          │
             │                 └──────────────────────────┘
             ▼                   ▲
┌──────────────────────────┐     │
│ ASP page creates link to │─────┘
│ view page in full        │
└──────────────────────────┘
```

Results: -

Adding diagrams to your planning is essential as you can get easily lost within a website and forget what each page is supposed to be doing. The user will actually be creating files, then they can edit their own files, and anyone will be able to see them. There are various reasons a user may use this type of script, it could be for a recipe website or even a dating website!

The other way that ASP can be used is if all the information is stored in a database, this is explained further on in the book (Day 4).

If you have any problems with file permisions you may need to see 'Day 4, Folder permisions' (page 84-85). This deals with the permissions wizard that may be part of your problem.

This type of coding can be useful to store a users in formation or just notes that can be easily retrieved. You could even enable people to write web pages in HTML by using this method and they could instantly see there creation as it would be online, instead of creating a .txt file it would be a .html file, or even an .asp file.

Creating text files

Createfile.asp

```
<% set myfile = server.createobject("scripting.filesystemobject")
set mytextstream = myfile.createtextfile
("c:\inetpub\wwwroot\book\day2\mikesfile.txt")
%>
```
This part above is creating the text file from last page........

```
<big>You have now created a file in the root called mikesfile.txt<p>
If you reload this page, it will not create another because it
already<br> has a file called "mikesfile.txt"
<p>
<a href="openfile.asp">Open the file ready to write to it</a><p>
```

**This part above is setting up the next page, creating the
onscreen text and link to next page.........**

Results: -

Back ▾ ❌ 🔄 🏠 🔍 Search ⭐ Favorites 📧 🖨 W ▾

Address http://mikes/book/day2/createfile.asp

You have now created a file in the root called mikesfile.txt

If you reload this page, it will not create another because it already
has a file called "mikesfile.txt"

Open the file ready to write to it

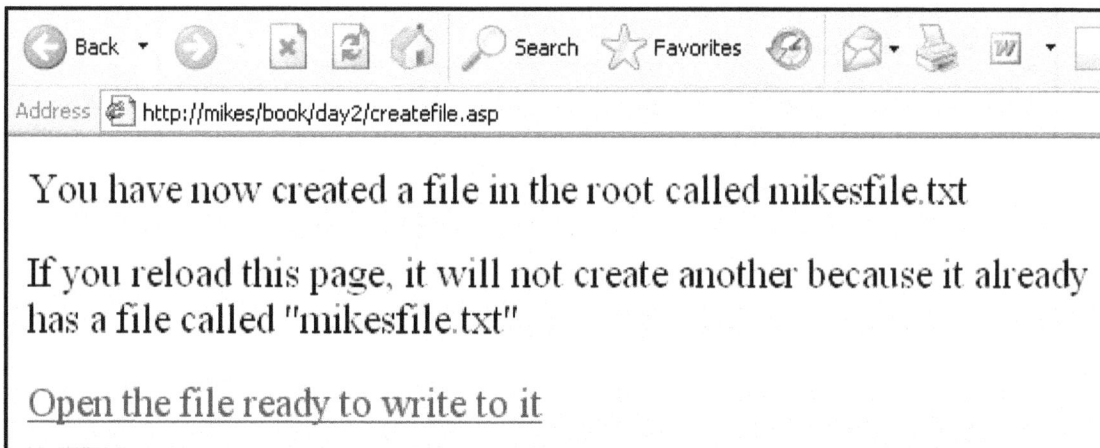

✎ We can see that the file that was created, is in a folder that we
chose by the url. Check with your hosting provider that they will
allow the creation of certain files on their servers. It will be fine
to host locally, as long as all of your permissions are set
correctly.

✎ In the second page after clicking the link it has now created a
text file that has been given a file name that was hard coded.
Study the code to see how this was done.

Adding data to a text file

Openfile.asp

```
<% set myfile = server.createobject("scripting.filesystemobject")
set mytextstream = myfile.opentextfile
("c:\inetpub\wwwroot\book\day2\mikesfile.txt")%>
This has now opened the text file that we just created, but of course
we have not output it to the screen.<p>
There would be no use just yet as there is nothing in the file.
<p><a href="adddata.asp">Lets add some data</a>

This next part opens and writes the first line
<% set myfile = server.createobject("scripting.filesystemobject")
set mytextstream = myfile.opentextfile
("c:\inetpub\wwwroot\book\day2\mikesfile.txt", 2)
mytextstream.writeline("This is the firstline of my text")
mytextstream.close
%>
```

Results: -

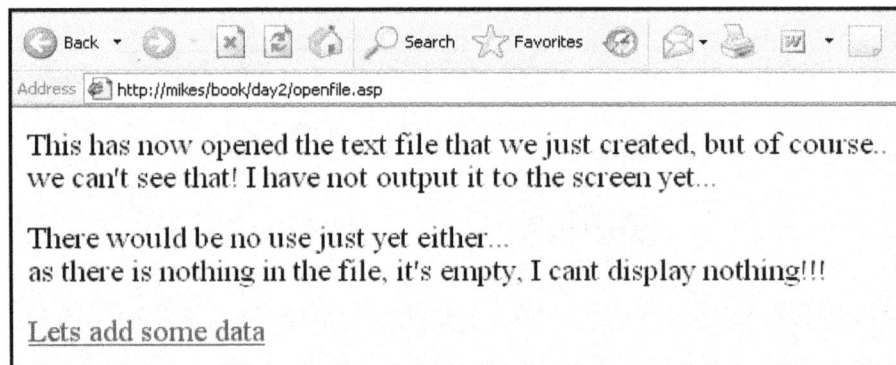

This has now opened the text file that we just created, but of course..
we can't see that! I have not output it to the screen yet...

There would be no use just yet either...
as there is nothing in the file, it's empty, I cant display nothing!!!

Lets add some data

In the first script we have tried to open the file, which we have done but we did not output it to the screen. We would not notice this even if we had done this, as we have nothing in this text file!

The link takes us to adddata.asp which then adds some data to the text file (this is in bold above). If we revisit this page again it will only overwrite what is already there.

This is what the contents of mikesfile.txt looks like now.

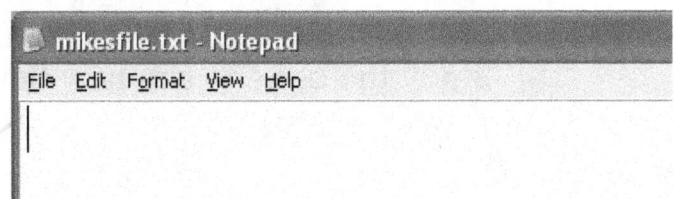

Adding data to a text file

```
<% set myfile = server.createobject
("scripting.filesystemobject")
set mytextstream = myfile.opentextfile
("c:\inetpub\wwwroot\book\day2\mikesfile.txt", 2)
mytextstream.writeline("This is the firstline of my text")
mytextstream.close
%>
```

The part above is writing to the file….

```
<big>This file has opened the textstream and written data to
the file<br>The number we have used to open the connection
is 2 <p>check the file to see the contents......
<br> It should have one line saying
<font color="red">
'This is the first line of my text'</font>
<p>Lets see what happens if we do the same type of open and
try to add some more text?
<p>
<a href= "addmoredata.asp">Lets add a second line</a>
```

And again above, the code is setting up the link for the next page.

Results: -

Back	Search	Favorites

Address http://mikes/book/day2/adddata.asp

This file has opened the textstream and written data to the file
The number we have used to open the connection is 2

check the file to see the contents......
It should have one line saying 'This is the first line of my text'

Lets see what happens if we do the same type of open and try to add some more text?

Lets add a second line

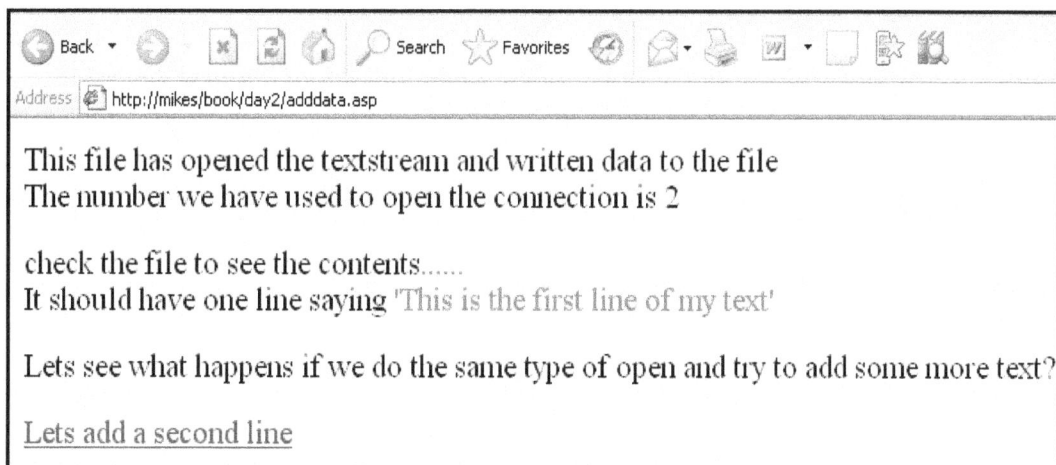

Here we see the contents of the text file as it is, at this present moment, take a look!

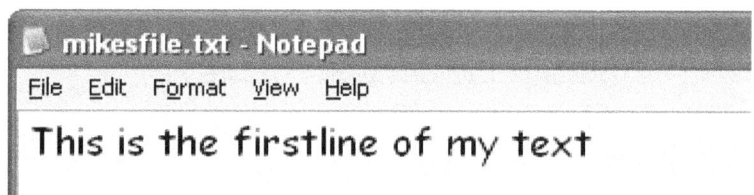

mikesfile.txt - Notepad
File Edit Format View Help

This is the firstline of my text

51

Adding data to a text file

Addmoredata.asp

```
<% set myfile = server.createobject("scripting.filesystemobject")
set mytextstream = myfile.opentextfile
("c:\inetpub\wwwroot\book\day2\mikesfile.txt", 2)
mytextstream.writeline("Hello this should be the secondline of my
text")
mytextstream.close
%><big>
There that should do it!<br>
Check to see if the contents have two lines of text?
<p>What ! <br>Where's the original line gone?<br>
Aaarrrhh I know what I did wrong,<br> I did not change the open
connection number to 8
<br>
Lets try again and add a third line<p>
<a href="addthird.asp">Add a third line.asp</a>
```

This number should be changed to 8 for appending.

Results: -

Back | Search | Favorites

Address http://mikes/book/day2/addmoredata.asp

There that should do it!
Check to see if the contents have two lines of text?

What !
Where's the original line gone?
Aaarrrhh I know what I did wrong,
I did not change the open connection number to 8
Lets try again and add a third line

Add a third line.asp

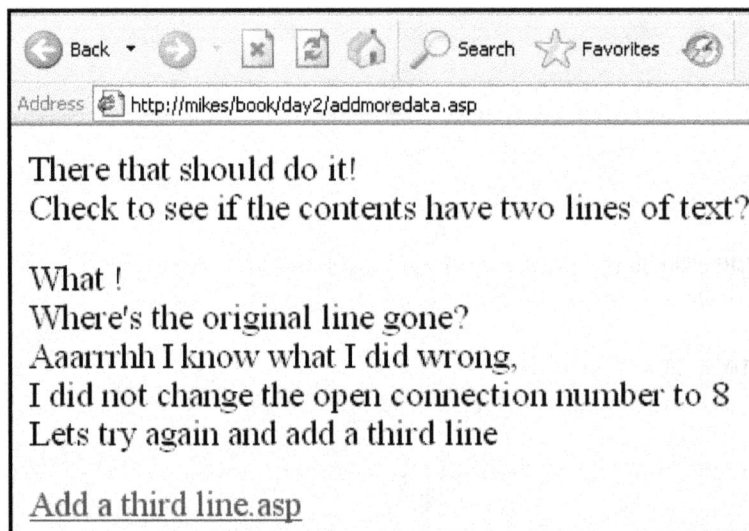

When we click upon the link this now takes us to a page that will add even more data. Problem, the first line has seemed to have dissapeared. When we wrote the text we should have used the connection parameter of 8 to append.

This is the contents of the file now.

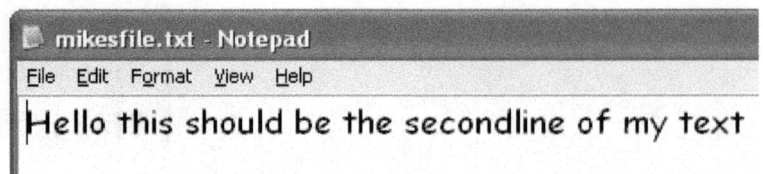

mikesfile.txt - Notepad
File   Edit   Format   View   Help

Hello this should be the secondline of my text

52

Reading text files

Addthird.asp

```
<% set myfile = server.createobject
("scripting.filesystemobject")
set mytextstream = myfile.opentextfile
("c:\inetpub\wwwroot\book\day2\mikesfile.txt", 8)
mytextstream.writeline("This should be the third line????")
mytextstream.close
%>
<big>
Check the contents now and we should have sucessfully
added the third line but <br>
don't reload the browser because it will append again and
again, and there will be lots of third lines!<br>
<p>We still have not read the file into the browser, lets try
that now<p>

<a href="readfile.asp">Lets read a file</a>
```

Results: -

Check the contents now and we should have sucessfully added the third line but
don't reload the browser because it will append again and again, and there will be lots of third lines!

We still have not read the file into the browser, lets try that now

Lets read a file

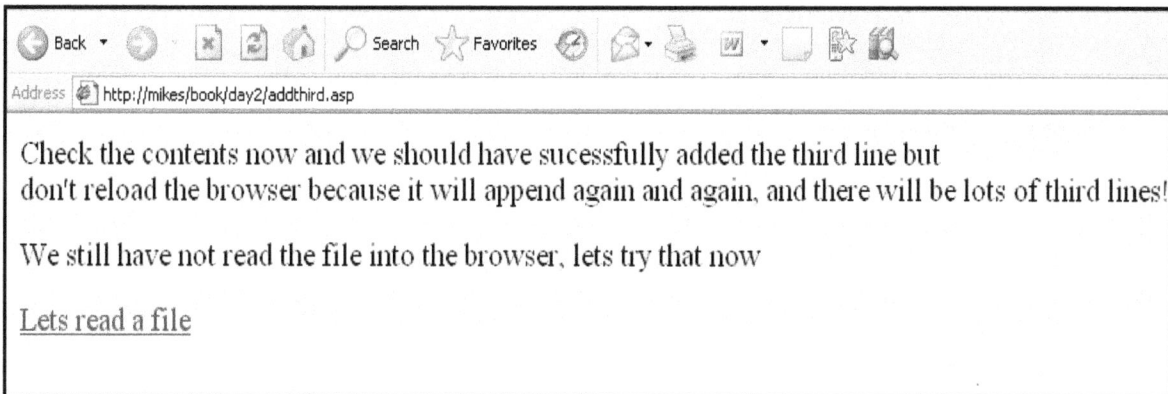

'Addthird.asp' has now added another line, but this time it has appended it. The actual file has now two lines, it has not concatenated the words. We then click the link and let the browser read the file.

The contents of the file are now these...

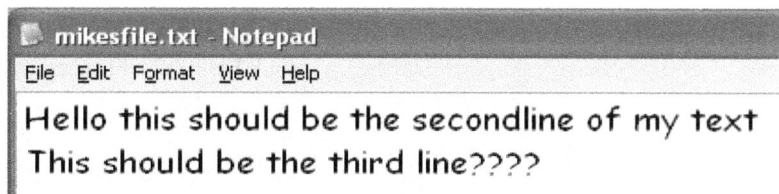

mikesfile.txt - Notepad

File   Edit   Format   View   Help

Hello this should be the secondline of my text
This should be the third line????

53

Reading text files

Readfile.asp

```asp
<% set myfile = server.createobject
("scripting.filesystemobject")
set mytextstream = myfile.opentextfile
("c:\inetpub\wwwroot\book\day2\mikesfile.txt", 1)
response.write(mytextstream.readall)
%>
<p><big>
You will notice that the file is read without linefeeds, making
it hard to read.<br>
Because I have used <b>mytextstream.readall</b> this will
read the whole text file into the browser.
<p>
<a href="method2.asp">Lets try another method</a>
```

Results: -

File	Edit	View	Favorites	Tools	Help

Back • Search ☆ Favorites

Address http://mikes/book/day2/readfile.asp

Hello this should be the secondline of my text This should be the third line????

You will notice that the file is read without linefeeds, making it hard to read.
Because I have used **mytextstream.readall** this will read the whole text file into the browser

Lets try another method

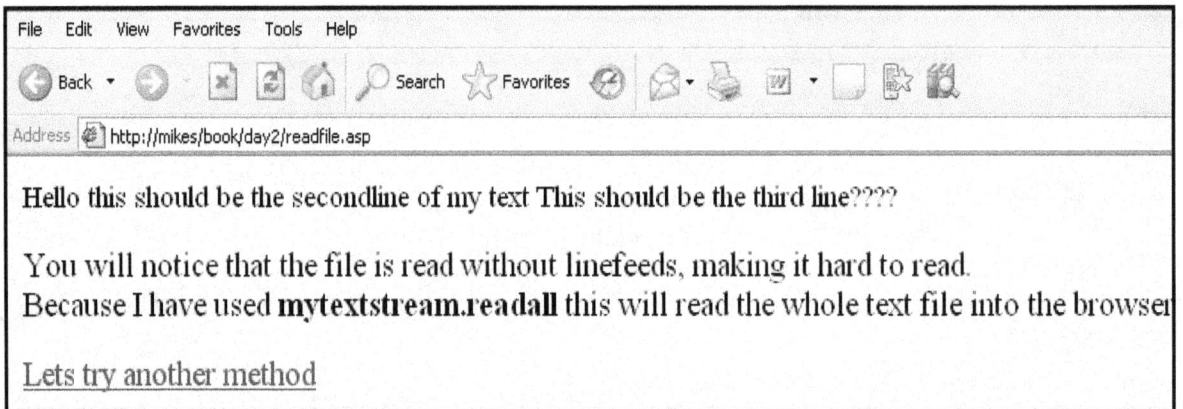

The contents of the file mikesfile.txt are now these as shown in the printscreen. Study the code and examine what it is doing, and when.

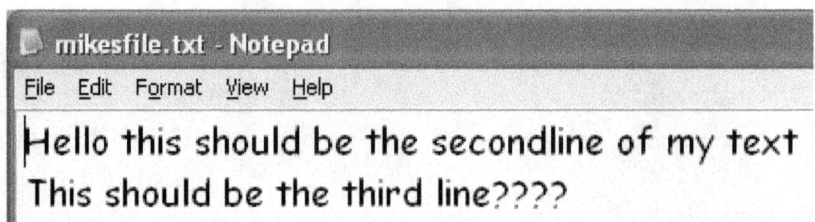

mikesfile.txt - Notepad

File	Edit	Format	View	Help

Hello this should be the secondline of my text
This should be the third line????

Reading text files

Method2.asp

```
<% set myfile = server.createobject
("scripting.filesystemobject")
set mytextstream = myfile.opentextfile
("c:\inetpub\wwwroot\book\day2\mikesfile.txt", 1)
response.write(mytextstream.readline)
%>
<p>
<big>
Because I have used <b>mytextstream.readline</b> this will
read only <br>one line into the browser, the first...
<p>
<a href="2lines.asp">Lets try two lines</a>
```

Results: -

File Edit View Favorites Tools Help

Back ▼ · ✕ · Search · Favorites

Address http://mikes/book/day2/method2.asp

Hello this should be the secondline of my text

Because I have used **mytextstream.readline** this will read only one line into the browser, the first...

Lets try two lines

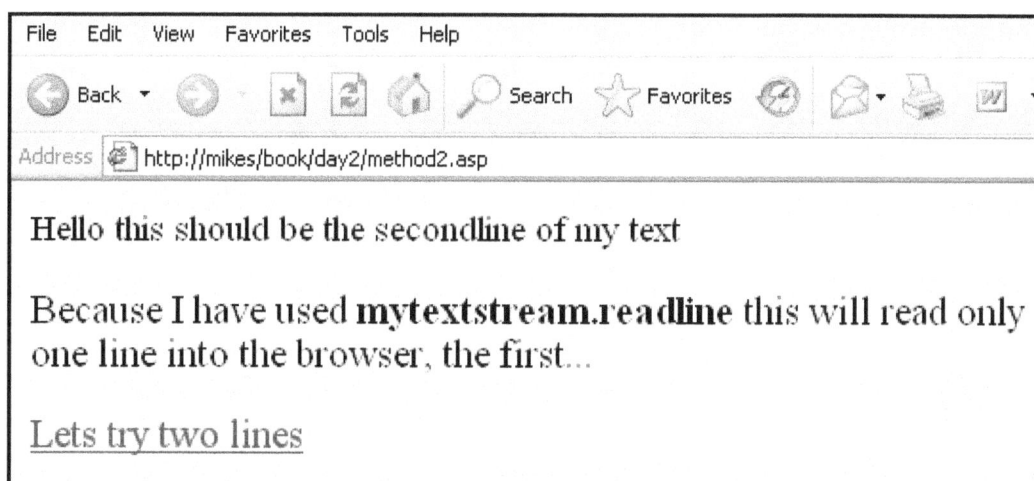

Method2.asp only reads the first line into the browser , but there are many ways of reading the text into a browser. Again below the contents at this stage...

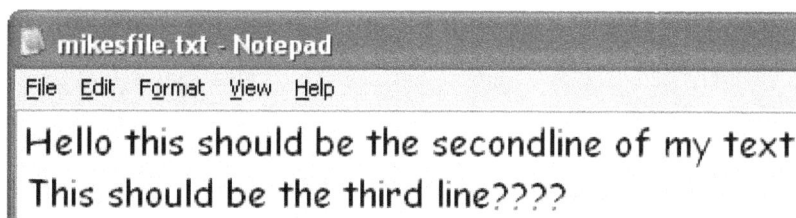

mikesfile.txt - Notepad

File Edit Format View Help

Hello this should be the secondline of my text
This should be the third line????

Reading text files

2lines.asp

```
<% set myfile = server.createobject
("scripting.filesystemobject")
set mytextstream = myfile.opentextfile
("c:\inetpub\wwwroot\book\day2\mikesfile.txt", 1)
response.write(mytextstream.readline)
response.write("<br>")
response.write(mytextstream.readline)
%>
<p>
<big>
Because I have used two<b> mytextstream.readline</
b>twice, <br>with a line break, this will read two lines into
the browser, one on top of the other.
<p>
<a href="characters.asp">Lets try just 10 letters</a>
```

Results: -

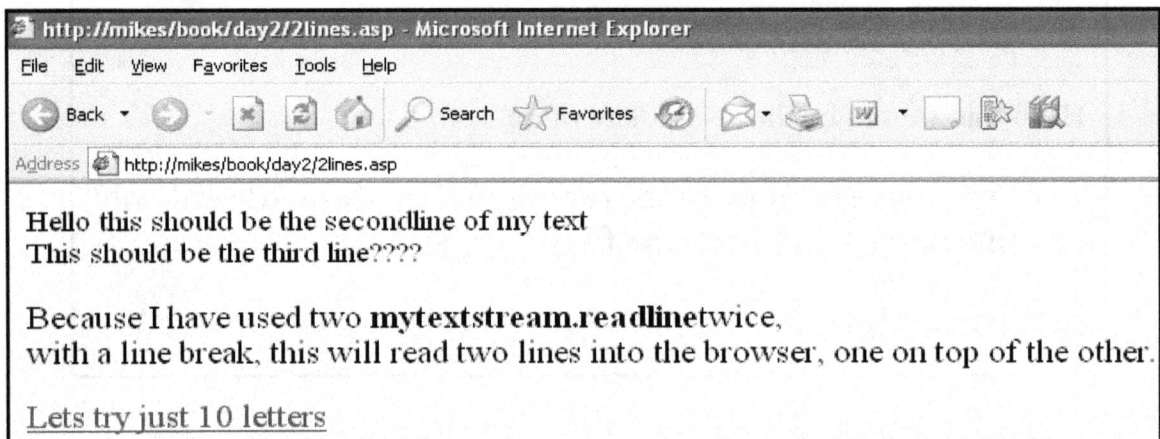

Hello this should be the secondline of my text
This should be the third line????

Because I have used two **mytextstream.readline**twice,
with a line break, this will read two lines into the browser, one on top of the other.

Lets try just 10 letters

2lines.asp reads in two lines, the first two lines of the
text file. (As you can see from the printscreen)

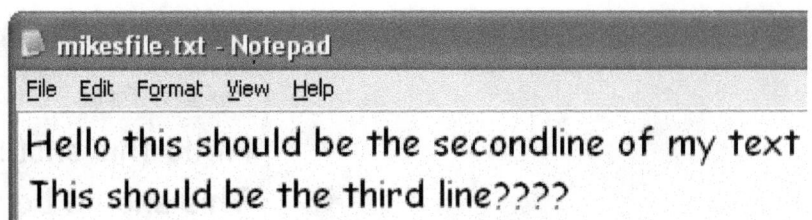

mikesfile.txt - Notepad
File Edit Format View Help

Hello this should be the secondline of my text
This should be the third line????

Displaying characters

Characters.asp

```
<% set myfile = server.createobject
("scripting.filesystemobject")
set mytextstream = myfile.opentextfile
("c:\inetpub\wwwroot\book\day2\mikesfile.txt", 1)
response.write(mytextstream.read(10))
%>
<p><big>
Because I have used<b> mytextstream.read(10)</b><br>
this will read just 10 characters into the browser.
<p>
Now comes the time to get rid of the file<p>
<a href="delete.asp">Lets delete the file</a>
```

Results: -

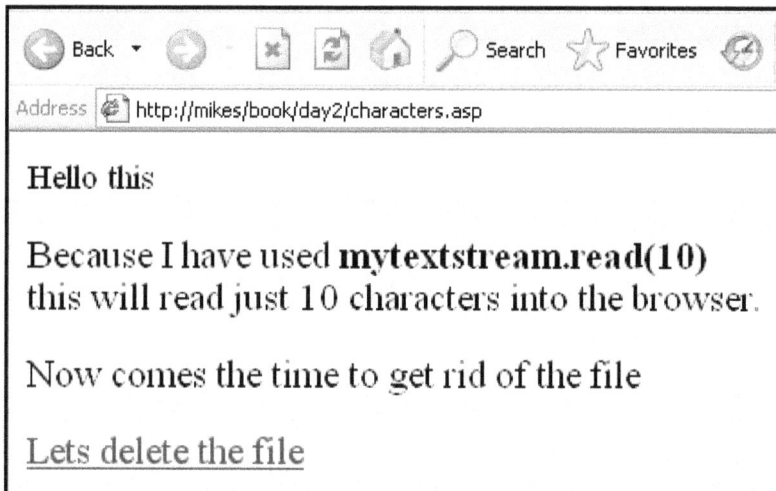

We now have a script that takes the first 10 characters of a textfile and reads it to the browser. We now have one link left, the delete link, once clicked the file 'mikefile.txt' should be deleted from the server.

Do remember that file restrictions apply and permissions should be set on the server.

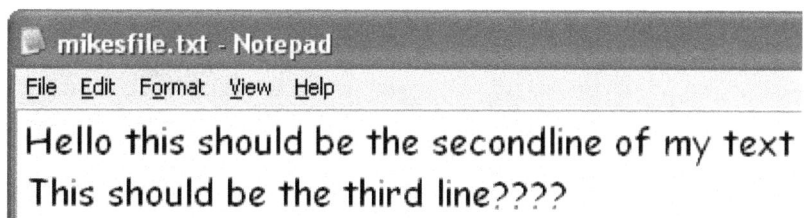

Deleting text files

Delete.asp

```
<%
set myfile = server.createobject
("scripting.filesystemobject")
myfile.deletefile("c:\inetpub\wwwroot\book\day2
\mikesfile.txt")
%>
<big>
Hooray, its gone or at least it should have gone. Check your
folder!<br>
If you reload this page it will cause an error because it is
trying to <br>delete something that is not there.
<p>
<a href="files.asp">Lets start again!</a>
```

Results: -

File   Edit   View   Favorites   Tools   Help

Back ·   Search   Favorites

Address   http://mikes/book/day2/delete.asp

Hooray, its gone or at least it should have gone. Check your folder!
If you reload this page it will cause an error because it is trying to
delete something that is not there.

Lets start again!

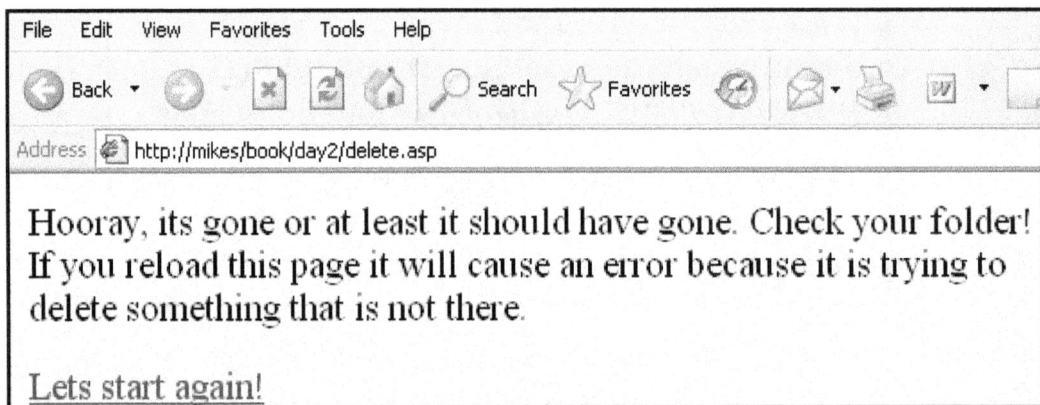

We now have no files, we have deleted it.

You can now use this script and build around this structure to extend the concept or project.

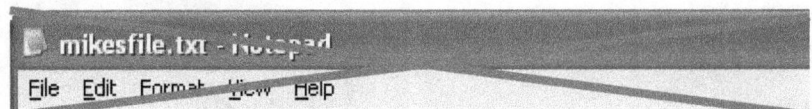

mikesfile.txt - Notepad

File   Edit   Format   View   Help

Creating a named text file

Choosename.html

```
<form action="choosename.asp" method=post>
Please choose the file name : -<input type="text"
name="name">
<input type="submit" value="add file">
</form>
```

Results: -

Back ▾   ✕ ⌕ 🏠 🔍 Search ⭐ Favorites

Address 🔗 http://mikes/book/day2/choosename.html

Please choose the file name : -[mikespage] [add file]

Choosename.asp

```
<% name=request.form("name")
set myfile = server.createobject("scripting.filesystemobject")
set mytextstream = myfile.createtextfile
("c:\inetpub\wwwroot\book\day2\" &name& ".txt")
%>
<big>
You have now created a file in the root called <font
color="red"><h3><%=name%></h3></font>
```

Results: -

Back ▾   ✕ ⌕ 🏠 🔍 Search ⭐ Favorites

Address 🔗 http://mikes/book/day2/choosename.asp

You have now created a file in the root called

mikespage

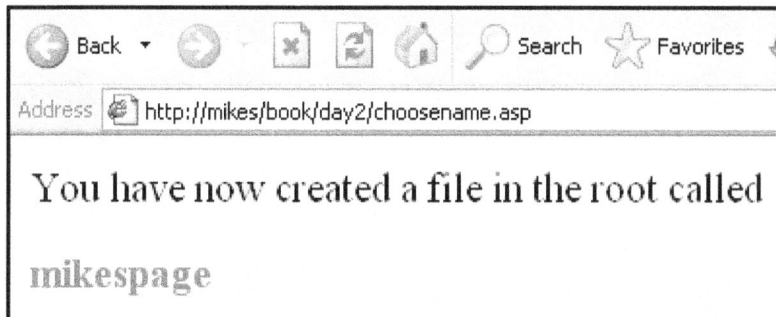

✎ As you can see, this coding now lets you choose the name for your own text file or even webpage to be created. You could further this program by letting the user edit the content.

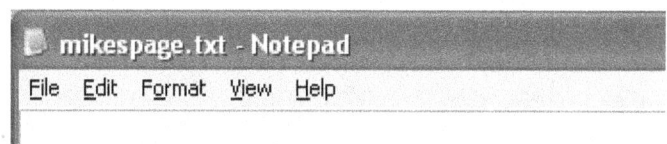

mikespage.txt - Notepad

File Edit Format View Help

Day 3

- ⇥ Dealing with Databases
- ⇥ Retrieving records
- ⇥ Putting them in order
- ⇥ Searching the results
- ⇥ SQL

This section deals with getting information from an already existing database. This could be a database amended by hand but seen through a web browser. Remember to close the database once amended by hand as it can cause the database to become locked and inaccessible by the web browser.

The example here I have chosen is a second hand car sales company, all that is needed is to show the customers viewing from home what cars they have in stock. This again can be adjusted to your own requirements when you understand how to use the code.

Database design

Connecting to a Database

The design of a database is very important, it could be flat file or relational, it may have six tables, or use two databases with three tables in each. It is crucial to get the information first of what you want to create. Changing things later could, and probably will create confusion in all of your pages, and a total redesign will be needed. Remember to name files correctly too. It's just the same as changing your house foundations after your house has been built. Don't Do it!, get things right by starting out on paper.

Trial and error can be a lengthy learning process, so make sure you are proficient in databases, especially the file types and how a database can go wrong using queries. It may not be your coding that's wrong but just what you are telling the database to do! Programmers are not database designers or artists but we do our best...........

DSN Vs DSN-LESS !

Data Source Name (DSN)

DSN is the action of storing the name and location of a database you want to use and creating a link using a tool called ODBC, (ODBC is an open standard application programming interface for accessing a database.) but this can **only** work on the local computer. If you upload the website to a server online it will not have the same connection string to the database, unless it is setup again. Unlike DSN-less, this type of connection states the actual file path where the database is stored, so therefore when you upload to a server, all you need to do is you change one line in one file, (an include file) and the website should connect to the database you are using. (To find the correct path for the database you can you the 'Server Map Path' script which is shown on page 36.)

A database locally may have the connection string such as
(C:\Inetpub\wwwroot\book\day3\databases\cars.mdb)
But when uploaded it may not be on a C drive or in the Inetpub folder, therefore we change one line in the include file and from then on all connections will be using this location.

Tests showed that DSN-less connections were slightly faster than System DSN connections. I am going to make things simple and show you the easy way, after using this way, you will not have any reason to even attempt another way. But first, lets take a look at the hard way!

Database design

This is the confusing and difficult way, but we don't need to do this!

DSN-less connections are faster than System DSN connections, because DSN-less connections avoid a registry lookup. Below is what the DSN connecting involves, you **do not** need to do this, as we are going to use the easier way. (DSN-less)

System DSN connection.
Found in administrative tools folder: -

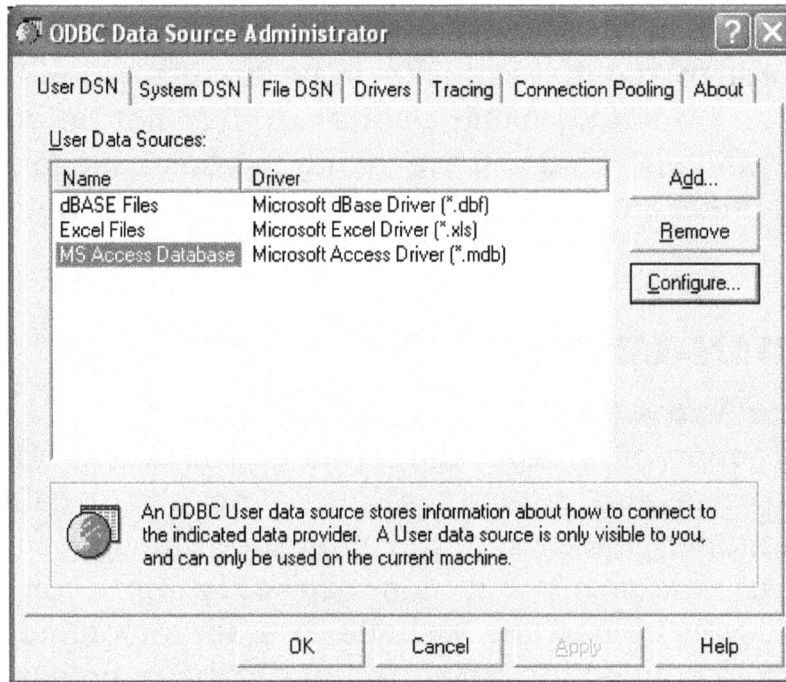

And again even more to set up !

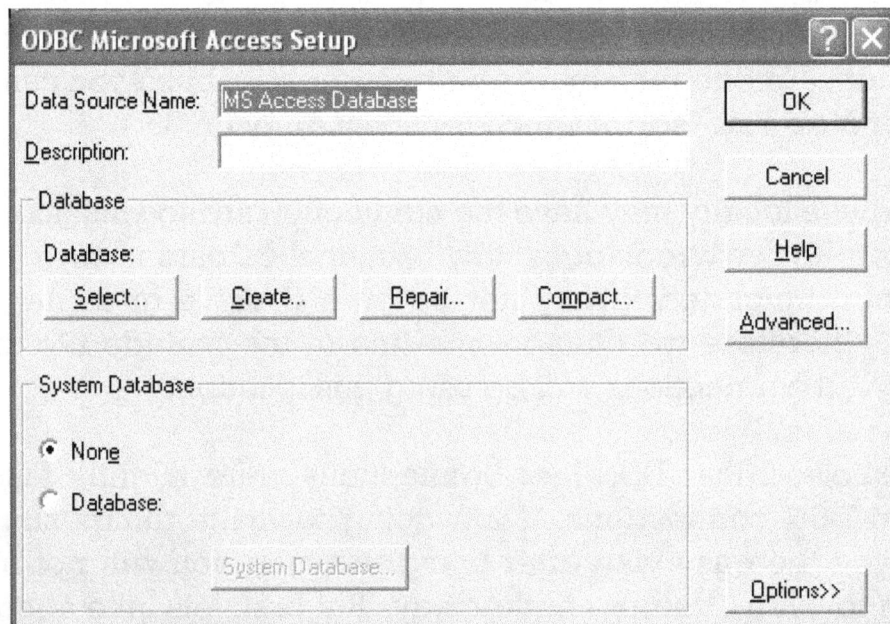

Making the connection

The first stage of processing data from a database is to connect to the database, this is done by using a special set of objects.

ActiveX Data Objects (ADO) is an application program interface from Microsoft that lets a programmer writing Windows applications get access to a relational or non-relational database from both Microsoft and other database providers. The ADO requires certain information such as the type of Database Driver, Buffer sizes, Threads, User IDs, Page and Database Timeouts, etc.

To link a database it must be ODBC compliant. (Microsoft Access is) Most of the major databases have created a set of common protocols that will allow them to transfer data between each other. These have Open Database Connectivity (ODBC).

Remember setting up the connection using DSN can cause problems such as: -

1. User access to the computer settings (uploading on an external site may have problems if the host does not allow DSN connections to be made.)
2. When you move the files and folders from one computer to another, it will not work, unless all connections are remade.

DSN-LESS CONNECTION (The right way!)

So therefore we are going to use a "Connection-less" DSN Connection String. First set up the name of the container you are going to use. In this case its called "dog" but it could be called anything. 'fish', 'sheep' etc.

This is the template of that connection: -

```
dog.inc - Notepad
File   Edit   Format   View   Help

<%
set dog = server.createobject("ADODB.connection")
conn = "driver={Microsoft Access Driver (*.mdb)};
dbq=c:/inetpub/wwwroot/book/day3/databases/cars.mdb;"
dog.Open conn
%>
```

Making the connection

set dog = server.createobject("ADODB.connection")
The ADO Connection Object is used to create an open connection to a data source. Through this connection, you can access and manipulate a database.

Again the '**conn**' is a string variable, which could be called anything.
This next line needs to be typed in EXACTLY as printed.
conn = "driver={Microsoft Access Driver (*.mdb)};

And now the path of the database to connect to.
dbq=c:/inetpub/wwwroot/book/day3/databases/cars.mdb;"

You now need to open the connection or make it active
dog.Open conn

Once opened the connection will remain open so when you have finished it is good programming practise to close the connection. (Save memory, processing space and possible corruption).
dog.close
set conn = nothing
(This usually should be placed before the end of any ASP script see page 89 for an example.)

We can use the Close method to break the Connection Object's link. If you forget to call the close method at the end of your scripts, ASP automatically closes any database connections that you may have open on the script exit of the session/page. The database can only have a certain amount of open connections and this will limit the amount of users at one time interrogating the database.

We now have a little trick, lets put this in an include file and forget about it....
When you need to access the database, just place
<!--#include file="dog.inc"--> at the top of the page, all we need then is the **SQL** to tell the database what information we need from it.

You will need the following file, it's important.
It will connect to your database. Save this file and keep it handy.
Dog.inc (here it is again as before)

```
<%
set dog = server.createobject("ADODB.connection")
conn = "driver={Microsoft Access Driver (*.mdb)};
dbq=c:/inetpub/wwwroot/book/day3/cars.mdb;"
dog.Open conn
%>
```

SQL introduction 1/3

What is SQL?

- SQL stands for **S**tructured **Q**uery **L**anguage
- SQL allows you to access a database
- SQL is an ANSI standard language

SQL is a Standard

SQL is an ANSI (American National Standards Institute) standard for accessing database systems. SQL statements are used to retrieve and update data in a database. This talks the same language as databases. SQL works with database programs like MS Access, DB2, Informix, MS SQL Server, Oracle, Sybase, etc.

- SQL can execute queries against a database
- SQL can retrieve data from a database (select)
- SQL can insert new records in a database (insert)
- SQL can delete records from a database (delete)
- SQL can update records in a database (update)

The table below is called 'people'

ID	NAME	GENDER	AGE	LOCATION
1	Mike	MALE	24	UK
2	James	MALE	35	USA
3	Marie	FEMALE	16	AUS
4	Lucy	FEMALE	50	FRA

<u>SELECT</u>
If we now write the SQL
'SELECT * FROM people'
This will pull everything from the table called '**people**' and produce all the cells as above, but if we write the SQL as
'SELECT name **FROM** people'
We will get: -
Mike
James
Marie
Lucy

Which of course is only the names from the table called 'people'.

Questions

If we write: -
SELECT name **FROM** people **WHERE** gender = '**male**'
The results will be: - Mike, James

If we write: -
SELECT name **FROM** people **WHERE** location = '**FRA**'
The results will be: - Lucy

If we write: -
SELECT age **FROM** people **WHERE** id= '**3**'
The results will be: - 16

If we write: -
SELECT location **FROM** people **WHERE** age= '**24**'
The results will be: - UK

The DELETE statement

If we write: -
DELETE FROM people **WHERE** name = '**Lucy**'
This statement would delete any row where the name is **Lucy**,

WARNING: - If you do not put the '**where**' clause in some statements, you may find your whole database gets deleted!!!

If we write: -
DELETE FROM people **WHERE** gender = '**male**'

We would have a table that looks like this now: -

3   Marie FEMALE   16   AUS

All but one has been deleted.....
Lets look at the update statement....

SQL has an easy to understand syntax (language style), read it carefully to see what it is saying. You will have lots of practice soon and can try it out when you have a database to test this on.

SQL introduction 3/3

The UPDATE statement
If we write: -
UPDATE people **SET** location = '**GER**' **WHERE** name = '**Marie**'

This means update the table **people** and change the **location** to '**GER' WHERE** the **name** is **Marie**.

UPDATE people **SET** location = '**SPA**', age = '**25**' **WHERE** name = '**Marie**'

This means update the table **people** and change the **location** to '**GER**' and the age to **'25' WHERE** the **name** is **Marie**.

The INSERT statement
If we write: -
INSERT INTO people (id, name, gender, location, age)
VALUES ('5', 'DEREK', 'MALE', 'FIN', '34')

We would have another record in our database, that has inserted the id as 5, the name as DEREK etc. That is not the only type of SQL we can do, there is plenty more! Look at these examples: -

The AND statement
SELECT * **FROM** People
WHERE name='derek'
AND LastName='johnson'

The OR statement
SELECT * **FROM** People
WHERE firstname='derek'
OR lastname='johnson'

AND OR combined
SELECT * **FROM** People **WHERE**
(FirstName='derek' **OR** FirstName='mike')
AND LastName='johnson'

Remember this is only basic SQL, enough to launch you into the world where it is used, but only enough so you know what's being asked of the database, nothing more. Now we can get to actually using it!

The Database

The database is the most important part of website you intend to create, as nothing will be output except errors if this is not correct. There are lots of errors to be aware of, check all of the following are done to reduce errors. My main top three errors are written below: -

1. **READ ONLY**

   Make sure you have the correct permissions to read/write to the database. Right mouse button on folder to produce properties. The **read only** box being ticked can cause problems when writing to the database.

2. **DATATYPES (database)**

   Make sure you use the correct data types (text, number etc) as if you are trying to input a number instead of a letter, then your coding will produce an error and you may change your coding again and again but there's not an error with it. You may find you have used the wrong data type.

3. **FILE PATHS AND FIELD NAMING**

   This can also be an annoying error, if the database has fields that in your coding you mention spelt differently. For example your coding its spelt "fnames" and in the database it is spelt "FNAMES". Do not mix upper and lowercase letters. Remember to triple check simple things because this is usually where the errors are found.

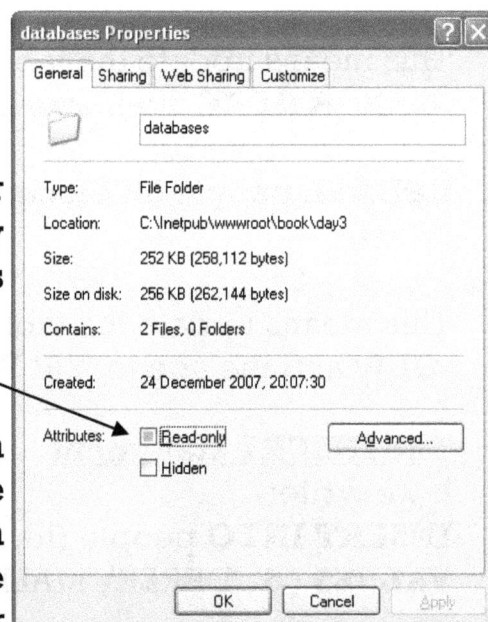

Structure of cars database

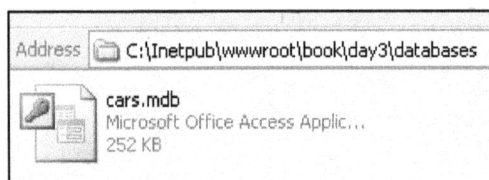

This is the basic structure of the database that you could use. There is lots of room to add and improve the ASP written in this book. Once you learn the basics you can start adding more complex and informative inquiries. This file is in a folder called 'databases', that is in a root folder.

Address: C:\Inetpub\wwwroot\book\day3\databases

cars.mdb
Microsoft Office Access Applic...
252 KB

Microsoft Access - [cars : Table]

File   Edit   View   Insert   Tools   Win

Field Name	Data Type
index	Number
make	Text
model	Text
Reg	Text
colour	Text
miles	Number
price	Number
dealer	Text
town	Text
telephone	Text
description	Text
region	Text

At the top of each script we use an include file.

We use it for the following reasons..
1. It simplifies the coding
2. If we change the name or placement of the database then we do not have to recode all the pages again.
3. It becomes more dynamic and acts like CSS.
4. Saves a lot of typing and hassle, as you use the same text over and over.

Study the coding on the previous page to understand what it does. These are the building blocks of ASP.......
We only need <u>four</u> files to create a full search of a database:-
1. The HTML or ASP page of coding (carsearch1.asp), we need this to create a search box that the user can add something to search for. This gets sent to our next page, 'car1.asp'.

2. The collecting ASP page (car1.asp), that retrieves the information that was sent in a variable called 'colour', is now changed to 'mycolor'. As you will see coding gets this information at the beginning of the script, as seen below.

    mycolor=request.form("colour")

    car1.asp is also used to provide the SQL that will tell the database what to search for.

3. Also present is the database connection string (dog.inc), this gives information to the coding using the include file method. We just use *<!--#include file="dog.inc"-->* at the top of each page that we need to connect to a database.
4. The database 'cars.mdb' inside the folder called 'databases'.

Files needed: -

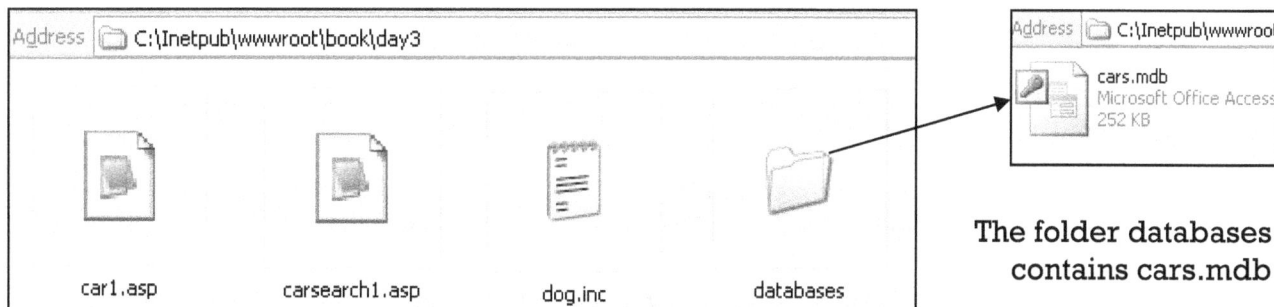

Address | C:\Inetpub\wwwroot\book\day3

car1.asp   carsearch1.asp   dog.inc   databases

Address | C:\Inetpub\wwwroot

cars.mdb
Microsoft Office Access
252 KB

The folder databases contains cars.mdb

Remember we only need four files to complete a search of a database, we now need to understand what SQL we use to search the database effectively.

Carsearch1.asp

```
<form action="carl.asp" method=post>
<B>Please enter colour of car. This uses a loop to display all re-
sults<br></B><input type=text name="colour"><p>
<input type="submit"></form>
```

Carl.asp

```
<!--#include file="dog.inc"-->
'Using the include file to get database connection information
<%
mycolor=request.form("colour")
'collect all data from field called "colour" sent from last page.
```

Record set →

```
SQLQuery = "SELECT * FROM cars WHERE colour = ' " & mycolor & " ' "
Set rs = Server.CreateObject("ADODB.Recordset")
rs.Open SQLQuery, conn, 3, 3

'This SQL statement says collect all cars where the colour is the same as the
'one typed in the previous page and stores the results in the variable 'rs'.

Do while not rs.EOF      'Continue if there are still more results in database.
response.write(rs("colour"))        'Write out result found in search
rs.movenext                          ' Move to the next record
Loop                        'Start again from the 'Do While not' line
%>
```

Results: -

Address 🔳 http://mikes/book/day3/carsearch1.asp

Please enter colour of car. This uses a loop to display all results

red

Submit Query

Address 🔳 http://mikes/book/day3/car1.asp

redredredredredredredredredredredredredredredredredredredredredredredredredredredredredred

🖎 Why do the results show in a long line?
Does this work with all the colours?

🖥 How can we change this to search for other fields?

🖎 *EOF* (EOF stands for END OF FILE)

Carsearch2.asp

```
<form action="car2.asp" method=post>
<b>Please enter colour of car.
This uses a loop to display all results</b><br>
<input type=text name="colour"><p>
<input type="submit"></form>
```

Car2.asp

```
<!--#include file="dog.inc"-->
<%
color=request.form("colour")
SQLQuery = "SELECT * FROM cars WHERE colour = ' " & color & " ' "
Set rs = Server.CreateObject("ADODB.Recordset")
rs.Open SQLQuery, conn, 3, 3
do while not rs.EOF
response.write(rs("colour"))
response.write("<br>")
rs.movenext
loop
%>
```

Looking deeper at the code.....

```
do while not rs.EOF
'starts the loop
response.write(rs("colour"))
'writes the colour
rs.movenext
'move to the next record in the database
Loop
'do it again till there's no more
%>
```

We go into more detail here, but by now you should be understanding how you are interrogating the database records, one by one, checking to see if they have something you are looking for, just as you would do by hand, except this time it's being done faster, by a computer!

When you have this working, change the code to make the script not work just to see what errors you are having. For example, take some speech marks out, recognise how it shows as an error, and remember it for future errors.

Carsearch2.asp/Car2.asp

Results: -

Without the <br> tag being added to this script, we would have the results shown horizontally, as we did in the last script. In this script each new result is knocked onto the line below.

It is done using HTML with the <br> tag, encased by ASP.

```
Do while not rs.EOF
response.write(rs("colour"))
response.write("<br>")
rs.movenext
Loop
%>
```

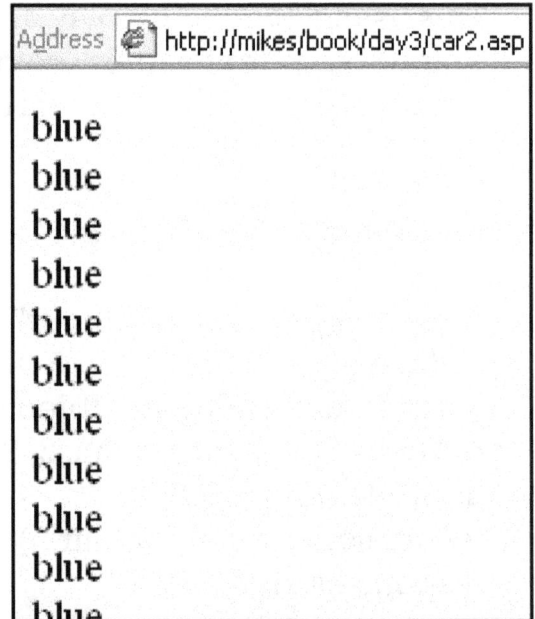

Address http://mikes/book/day3/car2.asp

blue
blue
blue
blue
blue
blue
blue
blue
blue
blue
blue

To make all the results return to the users screen we need to add in a loop. Below is the coding we used to get all the results from the database and not just one result. Study the coding to make sure you understand how it works.

Understanding the basics completely, is very important, don't move on till you fully understand this code. You will start to incorporate HTML widely into your scripts as you want to create tables with data inside, you will need to jump to HTML then back to ASP again, you will become more skilful of this as you practice. Try to create small projects and put yourself in a situation where you need to build such a website. They all need data to be stored or information to be found. This is where the interaction between user and computer needs to be clear. The HCI (Human Computer Interface) is very important. Being clear, precise and asking the user clearly what information you need in any one box on your form is very important. This is as important as the design of the database.

I'm sure you have seen some badly designed forms on websites, and probably typed lots of information, then every time you submit, it comes up with something you haven't done correctly....

Label text boxes with care....and make sure the box is named correctly.

There are a few other ways to make loops, this is only one of them. You must ensure when you have searched the database it has produced all the results available otherwise you may miss information, or it will be wrong. Test, test, test!!!

Carsearch3.asp

This script is a copy of Carsearch2.asp, the only difference is that it should be sent to carsearch3.asp instead. Copy the file and rename it, then change it.

Car3.asp (HTML version)

```
<!--#include file="dog.inc"-->
<%   color=request.form("colour")

SQLQuery = "SELECT * FROM cars WHERE colour = ' " & color & " ' "
Set rs = Server.CreateObject("ADODB.Recordset")
rs.Open SQLQuery, conn, 3, 3%>
<table>
<%do while not rs.EOF%>
<tr><td>
<%response.write(rs("colour"))%>
<td>
<%response.write(rs("price"))%>
</tr>
<%rs.movenext
loop
%>
</table>
```

Results: -

The script above now pulls the **price and colour** from all the files that have the colour blue in the field **"COLOUR"** within the database.

They do not look good due to the fact they are in a table **without** borders.

Address	http://mikes/book/day3/car3.asp
blue 3400	
blue 14500	
blue 750	
blue 12500	
blue 750	
blue 6799	

The script now gives us the knowledge on how to show other field names and use this with loops. The script should be nicely formatted and you also can see the structure of a table knitted into the coding. Make sure you include borders on the table.

See if you can now change these field names and add others , make sure you correct any errors.

Carsearch4.asp

This file is a duplicate of the file Carsearch2.asp, only this time it should be sent to Carsearch4.asp

Car4.asp (ASP version)

```
<!--#include file="dog.inc"-->
<% color=request.form("colour")

SQLQuery = "SELECT * FROM cars WHERE colour = ' " & color & " ' "
Set rs = Server.CreateObject("ADODB.Recordset")
rs.Open SQLQuery, conn, 3, 3
response.write("<table border=2>")
do while not rs.EOF
response.write("<tr><td>")
response.write(rs("colour"))
response.write("<td>")
response.write(rs("price"))
response.write("</tr>")
rs.movenext
loop %>
```

Results: -

As you can see this script shows borders, with borders you can now add colour to them. Shading them lightly will make it easier for the information to be read.

Address	http://mikes/book/day3/car4.asp
blue	3400
blue	14500
blue	750
blue	12500
blue	750
blue	6799
blue	7899
blue	6499
blue	6675
blue	14500
blue	4500
blue	7500

The concept of this script is still the same and runs in the same way, but the table structure is different as it is coded in ASP and not HTML. There are pro's and con's for this but generally it is down to the coders choice and only sometimes there may be a genuine reason of why one can be used and not the other.

Test out both ways and make sure you understand both, it may come in handy! Be careful of the speech marks and apostrophes.

Carsearch5.asp

This file is a duplicate of the file Carsearch2.asp, only this time it should be sent to Carsearch5.asp

Car5.asp

```
<!--#include file="dog.inc"-->
<% color=request.form("colour")

SQLQuery = "SELECT * FROM cars WHERE colour = ' " & color & " ' "
Set rs = Server.CreateObject("ADODB.Recordset")
rs.Open SQLQuery, conn, 3, 3
response.write("<table border=2>")
do while not rs.EOF
response.write("<tr><td>")
response.write(rs("colour"))
response.write("<td>")
response.write(rs("price"))
response.write("<td>")
response.write(rs("model"))
response.write("<td>")
response.write(rs("town"))
response.write("<td>")
response.write(rs("reg"))
response.write("<td>")
response.write(rs("dealer"))
response.write("<td>")
response.write(rs("miles"))
response.write("</tr>")
rs.movenext
Loop
End if
%>
```

Results: -

blue	3400	Pride	Plymouth	M	South West Cars	14000
blue	14500	LS 400	Inverness	J	Weldit Used Cars	56000
blue	750	Sierra	Liverpool	D	Wrights Quality Cars	29000
blue	12500	Accord	Nottingham	P	Sports Cars	12500
blue	750	Sunny	Maldon	C	Nippon Sales	23000
blue	6799	XJS	Portsmouth	M	Car-U-Like	109000
blue	7899	XJS	Middlesbrough	M	Dalton Car Sales	109000
blue	6499	XJS	Chester	M	The Car Shop	109000
blue	6675	Vitesse	Maldon	S	Nippon Sales	44000
blue	14500	Sunny	Edinburgh	P	Prestige Vehicles	40000
blue	4500	Cherry	Portsmouth	H	Car-U-Like	73000
blue	7500	Roadster	Middlesbrough	P	Dalton Car Sales	10000

Change some of the details on how this is displayed, or try to colour code each table column or row.

Add a column heading, this is very tricky, you only need to add this once, it cannot be within the loop.

Dealing with errors, EOF & BOF
(end of file & beginning of file)

Adding error control, edit car5.asp

Continued from original script car5.asp >>>>

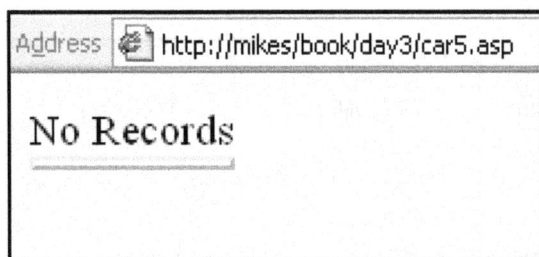

```
response.write("<table border=2>")

If Rs.BOF then
Response.write "No Records"
Else
```

If the recordset is back to the beginning of file, with no luck in finding results, the page will now write **"No Records"** You should then give the user an option to search again.

```
do while not rs.EOF
response.write("<tr><td>")
response.write(rs("colour"))
response.write("<td>")
response.write(rs("price"))
response.write("</tr>")
rs.movenext

end if
loop
%>
```

These outlined boxes are the new text that has been added to make this End of File error easier to understand for the user, and to prevent errors happening.

Results: -

Address	http://mikes/book/day3/car5.asp

No Records

Errors may occur if the database does not find anything so you need to say what will happen if this does occur.
The user needs to know also.
You could then redirect them to search again.

Remember testing again and again is the key to success.
So many websites have errors and if the data is shown wrong or searches do not happen as they should, this will cause you problems.

We now have an error checking facility in our files so that now whatever someone writes in the search box they get a complete answer properly formatted. You could even get it to say "Crimson was not found in the database" Try it...

Counting records

Count.asp

```
<!-- #include file="dog.inc" -->
'connection to database
<%
Set rs = Server.CreateObject("ADODB.Recordset")
'Setup container for recordset
sql = "select * from cars where make='ford' or colour='red' "
'tell the database our query in SQL
rs.Open sql, conn, 3, 3
TotalRecs = rs.recordcount
'the answer to our SQL in a number value is now assigned to
the variable name 'Totalrecs'
response.write "<br><b> " & TotalRecs & " </b>cars that are
either Ford or Red."
'write a sentence using the variable
%>
```

Results: -

Address http://mikes/book/day3/count.asp

194 cars that are either Ford or Red.

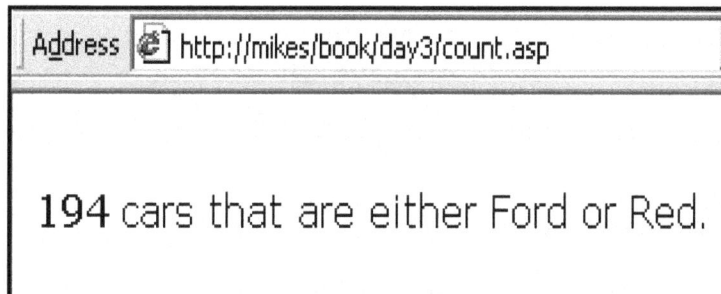

This seems easy enough to do, but we don't really want to check for all cars that are ford and red, we should do a separate statement for each. Counting records is a very handy thing to do as it helps to know the size of your database.

Adjust the coding so that it shows how many red cars there are and how many ford cars there are.

Try making the numbers red in colour and bold.
Try displaying how many of each colour car there is in one script.

SQL order

Sqlorder1.asp

This file is a duplicate of the file Carsearch2.asp, only this time it should be sent to sqlorder2.asp

Sqlorder2.asp

```
<!--#include file="dog.inc"-->
<% color=request.form("colour")

SQLQuery = "SELECT * FROM cars WHERE colour = ' " & color & " '
order by price "
Set rs = Server.CreateObject("ADODB.Recordset")
rs.Open SQLQuery, conn, 3, 3
response.write("<table border=2>")

do while not rs.EOF
response.write("<tr><td>")
response.write(rs("colour"))
response.write("<td>")
response.write(rs("price"))
response.write("</tr>")
rs.movenext
loop
end if
%>
```

Note: - The coding that displays "No Records" has been omitted from this script.

Results: -

blue	25
blue	125
blue	125
blue	300
blue	450
blue	550
blue	750
blue	750
blue	750
blue	790
blue	830
blue	830
blue	995

"price" is a field in the database, this has to be either a text or a number. (memos do not work)

You will notice that the prices have now been placed in order, so not only have the correct results been retrieved from the database, but they have been placed in order on the users page for easier reading.

Experiment with others to see the effect of this script.

Change some of the details to make other things happen as you want them too. Can you make it appear in order of two fields at a time?

Answer = No

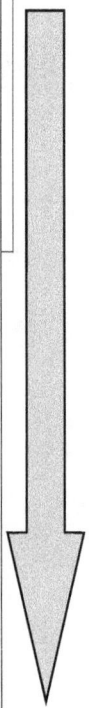

Sorting duplicates by SQL

Distinct.asp

```
<!-- #include file="dog.inc" -->
<%
Set rs = Server.CreateObject("ADODB.Recordset")
sql = "select distinct make from cars "
rs.Open sql, conn, 3, 3
%>

</b><font size=4>Choose your car</font> <select
name="choiceofcar" size="1">

<% Do While Not rs.EOF %> <option value="<% = rs("make")
%>"><% = rs("make") %></option>
```
*'This is the line that does the work, it places an option in the
select function, for every record that came back from the
query we sent the database.*

```
<% rs.movenext %><% loop %></select>
```
'and then loops till EOF

Results: -

The word 'distinct' means 'different from others'.
This is used to pick only one of each different answer and you will not get a duplicate.
This script can be then used to interrogate the models of that make, but that's another day!

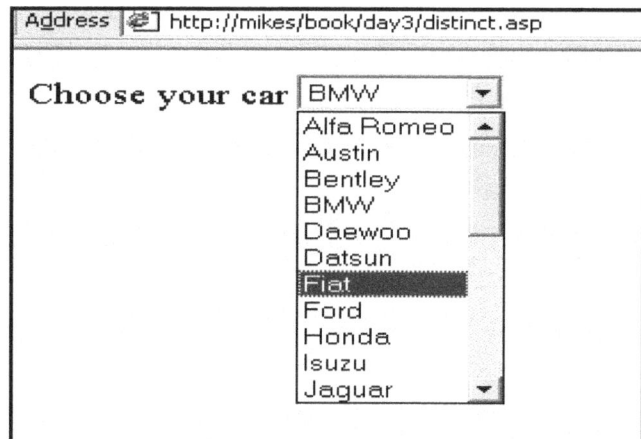

Address http://mikes/book/day3/distinct.asp

Choose your car BMW

Alfa Romeo
Austin
Bentley
BMW
Daewoo
Datsun
Fiat
Ford
Honda
Isuzu
Jaguar

This is a really time saving piece of script. Some people would hard-code this and write every make of car. As soon as we added another one to the database then the script would be out of date. In the way shown, we now have a self correcting page. We could let users add new cars to the database, and we still would be up to date with the way this script captures data. The SQL is doing all the work for us. SQL can be very useful.

Adding parameters in SQL to search

Doublesearch1.asp /

```
<form action="doublesearch2.asp" method=post>
<h1>Searching two fields</h1>
<B>Please enter Make of car. <br></B><input type=text
name="make"><p>
<B>Please enter Colour of car. <br></B><input type=text
name="colour"><p>
<input type="submit">
</form>
```

Address http://mikes/book/day3/doublesearch1.asp

Searching two fields

Please enter Make of car.

Ford

Please enter Colour of car.

Yellow

Submit Query

Doublesearch2.asp

```
<!--#include file="dog.inc"-->
<%
color=request.form("colour")
make=request.form("make")

SQLQuery = "SELECT * FROM cars WHERE colour = ' " & color & " '
AND make= ' " & make & " ' "

Set rs = Server.CreateObject("ADODB.Recordset")
rs.Open SQLQuery, conn, 3, 3
response.write("<table border=2>")
do while not rs.EOF
response.write("<tr><td>")
response.write(rs("colour"))
response.write("<td>")
response.write(rs("price"))
response.write("</tr>")
rs.movenext
loop
%>
```

yellow	1250
yellow	8000
yellow	1999
yellow	2100
yellow	2100
yellow	790
yellow	830
yellow	3499
yellow	9999
yellow	850
yellow	2380
yellow	3299

Results: - Note: This outputs only the colour and price, you can change what it outputs yourself.

Make this script show in order of price and when entering make of car use the drop down list by means of the distinct function. Start to build up all your ASP skills into one page.

Adding parameters in SQL to search

Colmax1.asp

```
<form action="colmax2.asp"
method=post>
<h1>Searching two fields</h1>
Please enter Colour of car. <br>
<input type=text name="colour"><p>
Please enter Maximum Price of car.
<br><input type=text name="max">
<p><input type="submit"></form>
```

Colmax2.asp

```
<!--#include file="dog.inc"-->
<%
mycolor=request.form("colour")
max=request.form("max")


SQLQuery = "SELECT * FROM cars  WHERE
colour = ' " & mycolor & " ' AND price < "& max &" order by price "
Set rs = Server.CreateObject("ADODB.Recordset")
rs.Open SQLQuery, conn, 3, 3
response.write("<table border=2>")
do while not rs.EOF
response.write("<tr><td>")
response.write(rs("colour"))
response.write("<td>")
response.write(rs("price"))
response.write("</tr>")
rs.movenext
loop
%>
```

Watch how the SQL is fussy, and has to have the correct speech marks in the right place.

Results: -   Colmax1.asp could be saved as a '.html' file, as it does not actually use any ASP.

Again a really useful script and one that you see many times on the internet and this adds to the user interaction on a site.

With all this information at your finger tips, have a go at changing the search criteria of one that searches for a price between two figures! Don't worry an answer is on the next page if you get stuck!

Adding parameters in SQL to search

Minmax1.asp

```
<form action="minmax2.asp" method=post>
<h1>Searching two fields</h1>
Please enter Minimum Price of car. <br><input type=text
name="min"><p>
Please enter Maximum Price of car. <br><input type=text
name="max"><p>
<input type="submit"></form>
```

Minmax2.asp

```
min=request.form("min")
max=request.form("max")

SQLQuery = "SELECT * FROM cars WHERE price > " & min & "
AND price < "& max &"  "
```

'This is the bit of SQL magic that does the trick, not only are we using <u>less than</u> but we now have <u>more than</u> too.
'We can extend this by placing the results in order as follows: -
```
SQLQuery = "SELECT * FROM cars  WHERE price > " &
min & " AND price < "& max &" order by price "
```

Results: -

red	300
blue	300
red	300
blue	450
green	450
white	450
red	450
grey	495
green	550
pink	550
blue	550
white	550
pale blue	550
pink	550
green	550
yellow	550
white	650

Address http://mikes/book/day3/minmax1.asp

Searching two fields

Please enter Minimum Price of car.

```
200
```

Please enter Maximum Price of car.

```
700
```

Submit Query

The search carried out was for cars between 200 & 700

You can adjust this script to output all information, such as make and model of car.

You should be able to build this script up, the SQL is the only difference, along with the variable names.

Try to add other parameters in such as '=>' (more than or equal to) and '<=' (less than or equal to).
You could even add another search box to really drill down to what the user is looking for, such as on auction sites and estate agents websites.

Day 4

▸ Adding records to a database
▸ Deleting records
▸ Editing records

This section is where most people see the strengths of ASP, in connecting to databases.

When would you use this coding?
If you want to keep an online data database where employees can see stock, and add to it. Maybe an estate agents, library, DVD shop or any type of stock, there are so many opportunities for this type of coding to be used. Used in conjunction with the rest of the scripts you can build up quite a powerful website...

Folder permissions and rights

Adding data to a database is fairly straightforward.
There are a few things you should note for this procedure.

Getting data to display is easy, but when you have to change the data upon a server the server does not like anyone doing this, and may stop you from doing so.

This is where permissions come in to the equation. Being good at programming isn't good enough when using ASP. You need to know your way round the server, and not just one server.
To make this as easy as possible I have not made this for any particular operating system, and have checked everything on systems running Windows Vista and Windows XP Professional. Don't try this on Windows XP home as it does not have all the requirements to run ASP. There are ways of doing this but you will need to run third party server software, and it can be different in every case.

When migrating any ASP site from one server to another you must be aware of two things: -

1.   Your DSN paths will change and scripts like 'dog.inc' which we have used as an include file will now point to folders that may not be there or they may have changed, and will need to be corrected.

2.   The permissions set on folders will also may be wrong, and if you come across errors like 'updateable queries need to be used' etc. when moving sites, check the folders are not just read only. As you can see here this folder would not be allowed to write data to the database inside the folder as it is read only.

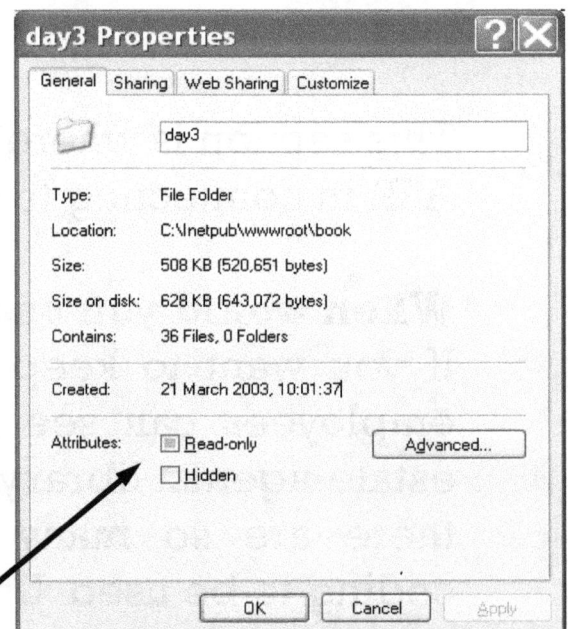

day3 Properties	? X
General	Sharing	Web Sharing	Customize

day3

Type:	File Folder
Location:	C:\Inetpub\wwwroot\book
Size:	508 KB (520,651 bytes)
Size on disk:	628 KB (643,072 bytes)
Contains:	36 Files, 0 Folders

Created: 21 March 2003, 10:01:37

Attributes: ☐ Read-only   [Advanced...]
☐ Hidden

[OK] [Cancel] [Apply]

Correcting errors

Remember there is a lot of help out there, sometimes too much!

The biggest pain or worst nightmare is when you get an error in ASP.
90% of the time it is an error with coding.
5% of the time it is with permissions.
4% of the time it is file paths being wrong, and the last 1% is usually the ones you get, this will need research!
(Try typing the error code in a search engine)
The screen dump shown here shows a very common error.
It states the operation must be an updateable query. This again leads us to file permissions. Instead of setting all folders to NOT read only, we can do this for all sites in one swift move, and it usually fixes this error.

Technical Information (for support personnel)

- Error Type:
  Microsoft OLE DB Provider for ODBC Drivers (0x80004005)
  [Microsoft][ODBC Microsoft Access Driver] Operation must use an updateable query.
  /book/day3/add2.asp, line 35

- Browser Type:
  Mozilla/4.0 (compatible; MSIE 6.0; Windows NT 5.1; SV1; .NET CLR 1.1.4322; .NET CLR 2.0.50727; .NET CLR 3.0.04506.30)

- Page:
  POST 30 bytes to /book/day3/add2.asp

- POST Data:
  idno=33&fname=mike&sname=young

In the control panel, open administrative tools, Internet Information Services, and you will see the screen opposite.

Expand the tree till you get to permissions wizard and go through this procedure.

Retry your problem and with luck your problem will have disappeared. If not try looking at your code.

Note:- Cutting and pasting into notepad can cause certain characters such as speech marks and the occasional apostrophe to show differently.

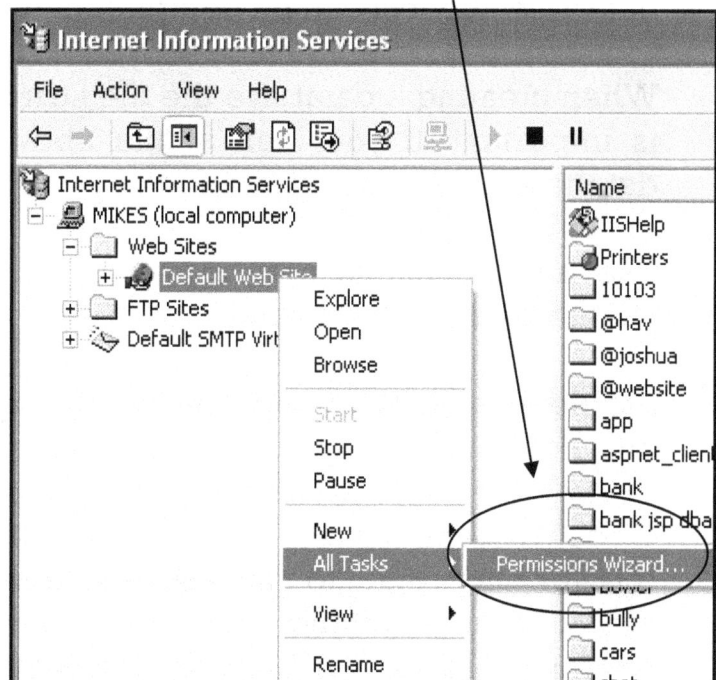

Internet Information Services

File   Action   View   Help

Internet Information Services
  MIKES (local computer)
    Web Sites
      Default Web Site
    FTP Sites
    Default SMTP Virt

Explore
Open
Browse
Start
Stop
Pause
New
All Tasks
View
Rename

Permissions Wizard...

Name
IISHelp
Printers
10103
@hav
@joshua
@website
app
aspnet_client
bank
bank jsp dba
bully
cars
chat

85

Adding data to a database 1/4

Files needed for creating an online database are shown below.

You will eventually build up all of these files. You will start with Add1.asp on the next page.

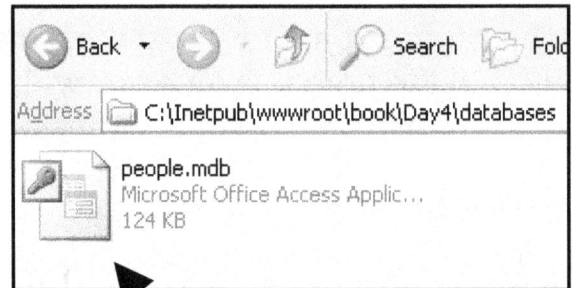

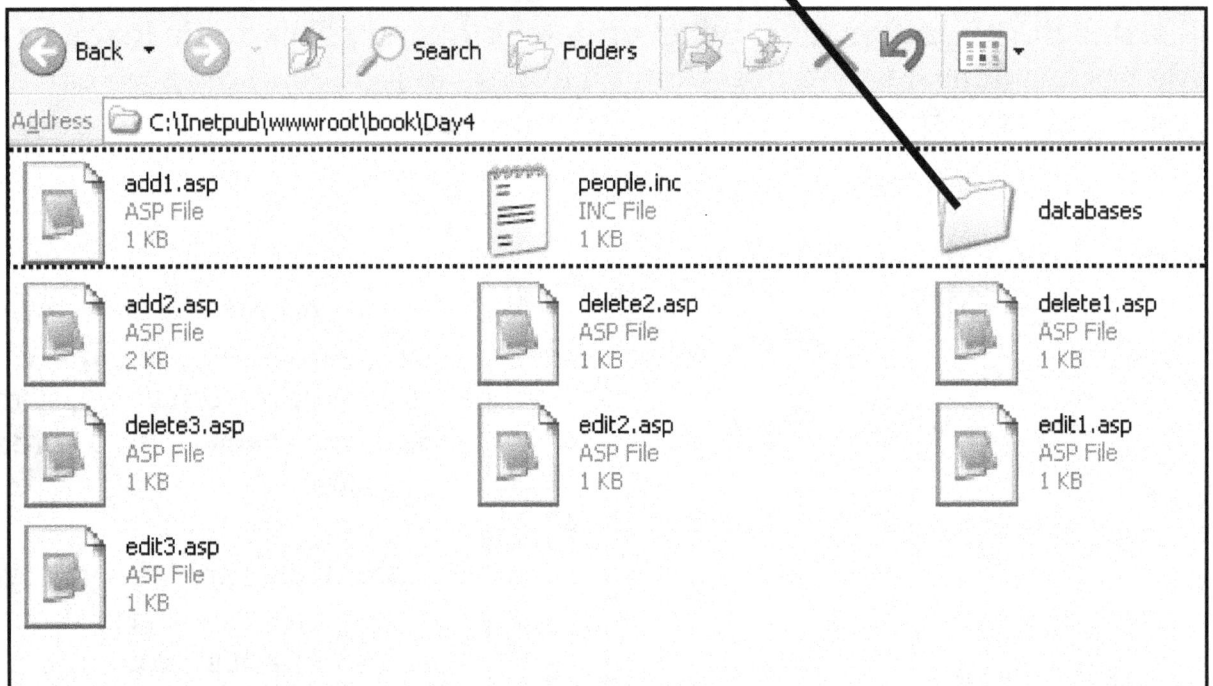

Back ▾				Search	Fol

Address: C:\Inetpub\wwwroot\book\Day4\databases

people.mdb
Microsoft Office Access Applic...
124 KB

Back ▾			Search	Folders				

Address: C:\Inetpub\wwwroot\book\Day4

add1.asp	people.inc	databases
ASP File	INC File	
1 KB	1 KB	

add2.asp	delete2.asp	delete1.asp
ASP File	ASP File	ASP File
2 KB	1 KB	1 KB

delete3.asp	edit2.asp	edit1.asp
ASP File	ASP File	ASP File
1 KB	1 KB	1 KB

edit3.asp
ASP File
1 KB

You do not need all of the files to start practising and testing. You only need one '.asp' file, one include file and a folder that contains a database, the rest can be completed at a later date.

When creating a database the file structure you have in your directory is important. If you look at the above screenshot you can see the database is in a separate directory called databases.

The include file is next to all of the other files so it can be used whenever a file calls for it.

Problems usually arise from files being in the wrong place and/or a mistake from writing the wrong path.

Once you have the directory as above you are ready to start creating.
It is very important to make sure your 'include file' points to the correct place. If not, nothing will work. The servermappath script shown earlier (page 34), will help you if you cant quite find the correct path.

Create a new folder called day4, save all of the scripts inside.

Add1.asp

After all of the worries about permissions are over, we can get to the coding. We start with a simple HTML search page.

```
<form action="add2.asp" method=post>
<h1>Adding to a database</h1>
<b>Please enter ID number.</b><br>
<input type=text name="idno"><p>
<b>Please enter First name.</b><br>
<input type=text name="fname"><p>
<b>Please enter Surname. </b><br>
<input type=text name="sname"><p>
<input type="submit">
</form>
```

This will create the following output.
When the data has been entered by pressing the submit button you will be sent to Add2.asp.

This page will show you what you entered, and then add the data to the database in one go.

Address: http://mikes/book/day3/add1.asp

Adding to a database

Please enter ID number

Please enter First name.

Please enter Surname.

Submit Query

The Database (people.mdb in the folder called databases)

You can create an empty access database with the following structure, without a primary key. (Yes you need to know databases quite well to be skilled in using ASP!)
The table should be called **'people.mdb'**.

Field Name	Data Type
idno	Number
fname	Text
sname	Text

people : Table

Eventually this database will start to get filled by what we enter into the text boxes.

You may get errors such as the database does not like duplicates, you may get **data type** errors meaning your placing a number in a text box, when actually you should be placing a letter. This can happen vice-versa. Sometimes having an example in the database to start with helps. Remember try to use lowercase, it just makes things easier with less errors to correct.

Adding data to a database 3/4

People.inc

```
<%
set dog = server.createobject("ADODB.connection")
conn = "driver={Microsoft Access Driver (*.mdb)}; dbq=c:/inetpub/
wwwroot/book/day4/databases/people.mdb;"
dog.Open conn
%>
```

Add2.asp

This is the ASP page, not the simple HTML page.
This coding is structured in a table.

```
<!-- #include file="people.inc" -->
<%
response.buffer=true
```

Connection to database made, and response.buffer speeds up site and makes sure it completes the search and displays before doing anything else.

```
fname = Request.Form("fname")
sname = Request.Form("sname")
idno = Request.Form("idno")
```

Getting the variables from last page that were passed...

```
response.write(" <p>")
response.write("<table><tr><td>")
response.write("FIRST NAME:  ")
response.write("<td>")
response.write(fname)
response.write("</tr>")
response.write("<tr><td>")
response.write("SURNAME:  ")
response.write("<td>")
response.write(sname)
response.write("</tr>")
response.write("<tr><td>")
response.write("ID NUMBER:  ")
response.write("<td>")
response.write(idno)
response.write("</tr></table><br>")
```

Standard coding to display the Information entered on Add1.asp in a table.

Continued on next page........

Adding data to a database 4/4

Add2.asp *continued...*

This is the bit that does all the work........

Dim strSQL ◄———— Resets a variable

Searches for duplicates

strSQL = "SELECT * FROM people WHERE idno = "& idno &" "
Set rsa = Server.CreateObject("ADODB.Recordset")
rsa.Open strSQL, conn, 3, 3

If rsa.EOF Then ◄———— If end of file reached and none found carry on

SQL states values that go into database….

SQL = "**INSERT INTO** people(**idno,fname,sname**) VALUES
(' "&**idno**&" ',' "&**fname**&" ',' "&**sname**&" ')"
Set rs = Server.CreateObject("ADODB.Recordset")
rs.Open SQL, conn, 3, 3 ◄———— Opens the database and inserts records

response.write("THESE DETAILS HAVE BEEN
SUBMITTED TO THE
DATABASE <p><a href='add1.asp.'>Home</a>")

else ◄———— If you do find duplicates then do this...
response.Write
("<h2><font color='red'>Record exists</font></h2>")
response.write("<a href='add1.asp'>or click here to start again</a>")
End If

dog.close ◄———— Close connection, the more connections
closed more people can access the database
to get results.
set conn = nothing
%>

All of this should become clearer now...

✎ This script's job is to see if the ID number has been used, if not then add the record to the database. If there is already an ID number in use it will display the text "Record exists".

Check your database to see the entry....

Address 🔲 http://mikes/book/Day4/add2.asp

FIRST NAME: Mike

SURNAME: Young

ID NUMBER: 457

THESE DETAILS HAVE BEEN
SUBMITTED TO THE DATABASE

Home

Deleting data from a database

Delete1.asp

```
<form action="delete2.asp" method=post>
<h2>Delete file</h2><p>
<B>Please enter IDNO of <br> the file you
wish to delete.<br></B>
<input type=text name="IDNO"><p>
<input type="submit">
</form>
```

Delete2.asp

```
<!-- #include file="people.inc" -->
<%
idno=request.form("idno")

Set rs = Server.CreateObject("ADODB.Recordset")
SQL = "SELECT * FROM people WHERE idno=" & idno & " "
rs.Open sql, conn, 3, 3

response.Write("<h2>
response.Write(rs("idno"))
response.Write(" ")
response.Write(rs("fname"))
response.Write(" ")
response.Write(rs("sname"))
response.Write("</h2>")
%>
<form action="delete3.asp" method="post" name="m">
<input type="hidden" name="idno" value="<%=idno%>">
<input type="submit" value="DELETE" >
```

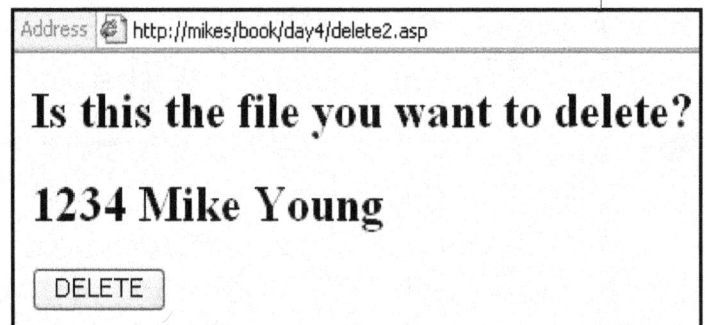

Results: -

> This script is <u>not</u> the final script, this script asks you to verify if this is the correct record you want to delete. It acts as a confirming script, you don't want to make mistakes when deleting data.
>
> When you click 'Delete' it will then send your hidden information to 'Delete3.asp'. This next script will do the deleting.
>
> See how the variable is passed in a hidden value.

Deleting data from a database

Delete3.asp

```asp
<!-- #include file="people.inc" -->
<%
idno=request.form("idno")

Set rs=Server.CreateObject("ADOdb.RecordSet")
sql =  "DELETE FROM people WHERE idno =" & idno & ""
dog.Execute(sql)

response.write("<h2>Record ")
response.write(idno)
response.write(" has been deleted")
response.write("</h2>")
%>
<p>
<a href="delete1.asp">Home</a>
```

Results: -

```
Address  http://mikes/book/day4/delete3.asp

Record 1234 has been deleted

Home
```

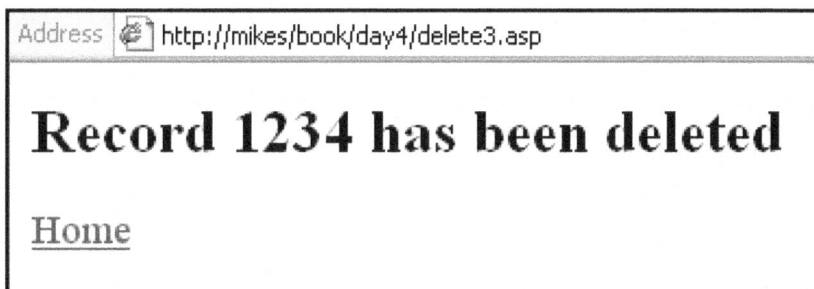

✎ This is a basic, easy to understand script that gets the re cord the user states they want to delete, asks the user to confirm if it is the correct record, and then executes the SQL to delete the record. Then it confirms deletion.

There is only one more script to understand before putting this all together, and that's editing the data.

🖥 When you get all of these scripts together you could write a page that combines all of these areas to create a complete company's online database using ASP!

Editing data in a database

Edit1.asp

```
<form action="edit2.asp" method=post>
<h2>Delete file</h2><p>
<B>Please enter IDNO of <br>the file you wish
to edit.<br></B>
<input type=text name="IDNO"><p>
<input type="submit">
</form>
```

Address | http://mikes/book/Day4/edit1.asp

Edit file

Please enter IDNO of the file you wish to edit.

[   ]

Submit Query

Edit2.asp

```
<!-- #include file="people.inc" -->
<%
idno = Request.Form("idno")
SQLQuery = "SELECT * FROM people WHERE idno = " & idno &  " "
Set rs = Server.CreateObject("ADODB.Recordset")
rs.Open SQLQuery, conn, 3, 3
%>IDNO <%=idno%><p>

<form action="edit3.asp" method="post">
First name<input type="text" name="fname" size="10"
value="<%=(rs("fname"))%>"><p>
Surname<input type="text" name="sname" size="10"
value="<%=(rs("sname"))%>">

<input type="hidden" name="idno"
value="<%=idno%>">
<input type="submit" value="Submit">
</p>
</form>
<%
dog.close
set conn = nothing
%>
```

Address | http://mikes/book/day4/edit2.asp

IDNO 1234

First name Mike

Surname Young   Submit

As you can see this takes a little more skill, not only do you have to get the results from the database and place them in editable text boxes but you also have to save them back to the database as well.

Remember keep things simple till you know it works and the design is also very important, as is your coding style.

Editing data in a database

Edit3.asp

```
<!-- #include file="people.inc" -->
<%response.buffer=true%>
<%
  idno=request.form("idno")
  fname=request.form("fname")
  sname=request.form("sname")

Response.write("<h2>Record has been changed</h2>")
Response.write(fname)
Response.write(" ")
Response.write(sname)
response.write(" is now record number ")
Response.write(idno)
response.write("<p>")
  ' Creating Recordset Object and opening the database
  Set rs = Server.CreateObject("ADODB.Recordset")
  rs.Open "people", conn, 1, 2, adCmdTableDirect
  rs.Filter = "idno = '" & idno & "' "

  ' Now updating records
rs("fname") = fname
rs("sname") = sname
rs.update
rs.Close
Set rs = Nothing
%>
<a href="edit1.asp">
Home</a>
```

Address http://mikes/book/Day4/edit3.asp

Record has been changed

Mike Smith is now record number 1234

Home

Results: -

As we can see from the screen shot, this record has now had the surname changed, and is now back in the database, ready for viewing.

The rs.filter makes sure we only change records that are the same as the 'idno' we are looking for. You can update whatever part of a record you want, you will need to just make sure the correct variable has been passed and include the correct coding.

Putting it all together....

The programming we have encountered in 'Day4' has shown us quickly how to create an online database. You will have probably encountered problems along the way, which hopefully, you have solved, and solving the problems is all part of being a good programmer. Understanding where the problems lie is important. Next time you have a similar problems you can use your experience to get you out of the problem. Make sure you practice often.

I find that creating a project for your self such as the ones listed may provide motivation to program in other ways using ASP.

When you have shown your ability in each of the areas needed for ASP which are adding data, deleting data, and editing data and of course searching the data, along with some passwords, time tricks and how to upload and control errors, you will be well on your way to create a complete online company database to collect information or subscribe to an email database etc.

Here are some useful ways ASP can help you by integrating a database into your website: -

- As a way of subscribing to a website, ready to use the database for email accounts to email out. You could let the user delete them self from the database if they wish.
- A company could use this to add stock to a database without the database being installed on there own computer, others could also check stock. (Like the car company example)
- An updatable telephone/contact directory
- An automatic appointment creator, (I have used this for parents evenings, each student was given a code to book their own time.)

Many companies use ASP programming, and you will see many examples of this as you visit various websites. Adding other languages will make the website easier and more presentable to the user. In any webpage designed you will normally find the following languages: -

JavaScript for the control over text boxes, making sure the user fills out the text boxes as they should (error correction).

CSS to enable the style of the web page to be the same throughout and other little hacks and tricks.

HTML for the simple stuff and the main layout.

ASP of course!, to make the integration of a database possible.

Notes....

If you want to improve your web skills further than HTML, look no further than ASP. This book covers the basics of Active Server Pages. Learn at your own pace.

Simplified...

Easy to understand scripts, each with a screenshot to help.

Basic...

Each script is only the bare bones, nothing more is added, the rest is up to you...

Easy...

You will be suprised at how easy ASP can be, learning a language can be fun...

What does it do?

Active Server Pages or ASP, is a programming language that can be used to search a database from a website. This book will help you create a fully working online database that you can adjust to your requirements. Along the way you will learn the many powers ASP has to offer, in small simple steps. When you have a website project of your own to build, ASP is a valuable tool in your web design skills. Its also quite fun!

Start now!

To start coding in ASP, does not need special software, no downloading, or confusing setup. You need only this book, and a computer running either Vista or Windows XP (professional).

- Installing ASP
- Handling Variables
- Passing Information
- Creating Text Files
- Passwords / Security
- Retrieving Records
- Using SQL to Search

£11.95